Suspicious
Packages
and
Extendable Arms

TIM DOWLING

guardianbooks

First published in 2007 by
Guardian Books, 119 Farringdon Road, London EC1R 3ER
guardianbooks.co.uk

Guardian Books is an imprint of Guardian News and Media Ltd.

A CIP record for this book is available from the British Library.

ISBN: 978-0-85265-087-5

Cover Design: Two Associates
Cover Photography: David Sillitoe
Text Design: seagulls.net

Printed in Great Britain by CPI UK

Contents

Health & Safety

Manners & Modern Life

Politics & Religion

Children & Animals

Business & Pleasure

Food & Fashion

Rights & Responsibilities

Crime & Punishment

War & Peace

The End

Preface

Everyone remembers where they were on September 11 2001. I was sitting alone in my office, trying to write a piece about bananas. At that point 9/11 was still destined to be for ever remembered as the day that the Libyan leader, Muammar Gadafy, offered to buy up the entire Caribbean banana crop in a grandstanding bid to liberate beleaguered growers from oppressive European and American quotas. Or so it was rumoured – no one really knew whether he had or hadn't, or whether he conceivably could.

Some simple arithmetic, however, revealed that such a purchase would provide every Libyan with 52lbs of bananas for the year – a pound, or about four bananas, a week. At the time your average European got through just 16lbs of bananas in a year. Russians managed just 10lbs. Meanwhile, Libya was already importing 20,000 tonnes of bananas, or 6.5lbs per capita per annum, from the Ivory Coast alone.

On the strength of these calculations, I was asked to write a short article suggesting helpful ways for the Libyan people to use up their onerous new banana allotment. I wasn't pleased, because such an assignment meant ringing up a load of nutritionists, chefs and food writers for ideas, and this in turn would require me to recount the whole unlikely tale to each of them, pausing several times to explain what was so funny about it. As I dialled the first number, I began to wish that some giant cataclysmic event would arise to eclipse the banana story so that I wouldn't have to write it.

As the afternoon wore on my resentment turned to panic. Nobody had returned any of my calls. The phone at the Libyan embassy rang and rang. I left voicemail messages on half a dozen mobiles, politely outlining my needs, but no one got back to me. What was going on? Why didn't anyone want to talk about bananas?

Eventually I received a call from the TV presenter and food writer Hugh Fearnley-Whittingstall. He explained that he had just stepped off a plane to find two messages on his phone; one from his sister telling him that wherever he was he should get in front of a television right away, and one from me, asking about bananas. It is perhaps a testament to the desperate, pleading edge I deliberately allowed to creep into my voice that he called me back first. We chatted for a while about the terribly small culinary window between a banana being under-ripe and over-ripe then he gave me a recipe for a banana milkshake. I was suitably grateful, mentioning how difficult it had been to get hold of anyone. We said goodbye, and he went off to find a television. About 10 minutes later, so did I.

My memory of the next hour is unreliable; I don't even remember at which point during the unfolding events I joined the millions around the world looking on. Did I see the first tower fall, or did it happen as I was carting the portable kitchen telly up to my office? I only remember sitting there in stunned silence, wondering what would come next, until it occurred to me that I still had not received official confirmation of the now inevitable cancellation of the banana article. I rang the person who commissioned it, and we exchanged a few cautious words regarding the precise extent to which nothing would ever be the same again.

"So," she said finally. "How's it coming?"

"You mean the banana piece?" I said. "Well, I thought, I mean it doesn't really seem to me like, at this stage, anyone's going to be too interested in bananas tomorrow." There was a pause at the other end.

"Oh, don't give up," she said. "That's just what these terrorists want."

I didn't know whether to laugh at that or not. I didn't even know whether I was supposed to laugh at it or not. So I just said "OK" and hung up. And then, with both eyes on the television, I wrote out 650 words about what the Libyans could do with all their extra bananas, using a quote from Hugh Fearnley-Whittingstall and a recipe for Bananas Foster that I'd lifted from some website.

Of course the piece didn't run the next day, or any other day; nor is it included in this collection, because, despite what some people say about every event, no matter how tragic or seemingly inappropriate, having inherent comic potential, certain things just aren't funny, and that goddamn banana story was one of them.

TD, July 9 2007

Health & Safety

Suspicious Package

Sometimes I read the Lakeland catalogue in the bath, but that's as far as it goes. I am not among those 23 million people whose homes, according to a recent poll, harbour an estimated £9bn-worth of useless gadgets, of sandwich toasters, foot spas and electric knives. I may occasionally wonder whether my life would improve if I invested in a container that kept my butter at the optimum temperature, but I know that most of these gadgets address needs that are themselves illusory. My philosophy is You Don't Need a Breadmaker, Because We're All Going To Die.

So when the postman delivered a large, bulky envelope the other morning, I treated it as suspicious. Inside the envelope was a box, which looked as if it might contain – or have once contained – a gadget, but I hadn't ordered any gadgets. There was no explanatory note, no return address: a breach of postal etiquette that struck me as potentially hostile. It could be anything – a letter bomb, a dead rat, a savagely mutilated doll. A person who orders a lot of useless stuff might open the box without thinking, but I had a bad feeling. I totted up all the times I had taken a controversial stand on a notoriously emotive issue: never. Even so, I called my wife.

"I didn't order anything," I said.

"Where is it now?" she asked.

"It's in the garden." There was a pause.

"You need something to open it with from a distance. Some giant, extendable arms." This is the sort of thing my wife says when she chooses to be part of the problem rather than part of the solution. After she hung up I thought about fashioning some probes using two broomsticks with a couple of forks taped to the ends, but I decided it would be embarrassing if for some reason the police then had to be called. "Can I just ask you sir," the officer would say, examining my home-made arm extensions, "what the thinking was behind these?"

When my wife got home she offered to open the package herself, but I rejected this option because I could not imagine an outcome that would reflect well on me. She suggested I open it using a dustbin lid as a shield.

This seemed a nice compromise between paranoia and recklessness. With the lid protecting my eyes, I teased open the box. Inside was a packet of throat lozenges. "Oh my God," said my wife. Beneath them lay an old-fashioned phone handset, snugly tucked into foam packaging. What could it mean?

The phone, according to the enclosed press release, was actually a stylish retro hands-free kit for use with a certain internet telephony service. The lozenges were an example of what passes for wit in PR circles. I'd need them after all the extra talking I was sure to do on a certain internet telephony service. My wife and I took turns reading the note until it sank in. "I was quite frightened by the pastilles," she said. She threw them away, just in case.

The phone went into the cupboard where we keep the broken video camera. I fished the Lakeland catalogue out of the recycling to see if they had any mechanical arms. Not that I would buy them. I was just curious.

Welcome to the NewsRoom at permachat.co.uk, the UK's premiere online current affairs forum!

>*connecting to server...*

Current Host: Chris2

Current Topic: A proposed series of strikes by firemen has been threatening to bring chaos to Britain. Should the government give in to big pay demands from vital public sector services?

Osama_bin_Laden: I support the firemen

mullah'omar: me too

capitalistpiglet: so you think they deserve a full 40 per cent pay hike?

Osama_bin_Laden: no I just want everything to burn down

mullah'omar: ha ha

Host_Chris2: omar and osama you are both sailing very close to the wind. Many chatters already find your usernames offensive

Bronco: they put a curse on me last week

Host_Chris2: your complaint has been noted Bronco

capitalistpiglet: I can't tell whether they're being satirical or not

Host_Chris2: permachat is watching for any breach of policy

Bronco: but my hair is falling out!

Osama_bin_laden: I forgot abt the hair well done mullah'omar

mullah'omar: its easy I can do boils as well

Pashmina has entered the NewsRoom

Pashmina: hey room whats up

Bronco: mullah'omar cursed me

Pashmina: are those 2 still in ere! Chris2 get them out NOW

Host_Chris2: I'm afraid I can't. Offensive usernames are only defined as those with swearwords in them

Pashmina: but they been cursin @ Bronco!

capitalistpiglet: perhaps it's a sophisticated parody of Western paranoia, but I just dont get it

Bronco: no they PUT a curse on me. My hair is fallin out!

Pashmina: I thought yr GP said that was stress from the call centre

mullah'omar: osama u still hiding in the same place

Osama_bin_Laden: yep. u?

Bronco: I quit the call centre. What does a boil look like?

mullah'omar: same place. seen any blasphemous films lately

Osama_bin_Laden: lilo & stitch

mullah'omar: yes I condemned it as well

capitalistpiglet: is it a political statement? Performance art?

Pashmina: I think their just kids messin about

Bronco: then how do u explain this huge lump on my neck???

mullah'omar: thats your head infidel

Osama_bin_Laden: lol

mullah'omar: got2 go osama. death to america bye
mullah'omar has left the NewsRoom
Osama_bin_Laden: bye
Host_Chris2: Who has a comment about the firefighters' strike?
Osama_bin_Laden: I just want everything to burn down

>connection to server has been terminated...

Rhymes for Insurers

Two medical students have written to the Canadian Medical Association Journal to complain about the representation of head injuries in nursery rhymes, which are often portrayed as "inevitable events that do not require medical follow-up". People who would describe this notion as "political correctness gone mad" have clearly never seen what can happen when an unsupervised infant is left in a tree-top, secured by a non-EU approved, bough-mounted harness. The best nursery rhymes were designed to be instructive, but few have been updated to reflect best practice in terms of safety or emergency medical care. All rhymes featuring head trauma must be amended thusly:

Humpty Dumpty sat on a wall
Humpty Dumpty had a great fall

Humpty Dumpty shouldn't have been
up on a wall without being roped in.
All the king's EMTs, who had heard Humpty holler
rushed to the scene with a cervical collar.
The king's paramedics were of the impression
that Humpty had suffered cerebral compression
but at casualty Humpty was happy to hear
it was only concussion, which is much less severe.
All the king's safety inspectors were baffled
when they saw that the wall had no railing or scaffold.
It only remained for all the king's lawyers
to compensate Humpty, and sue his employers.

Jack and Jill rode up the hill
with inadequate supervision
Jack fell down and broke his crown
in some sort of quad bike collision.
"Jack," said Jill, "you look terribly ill."
But it was too late to reprove him.
She knew that he needed emergency care.
But thought it was best not to move him.
So Jill kept Jack flat on his back
and helped him as best she was able.
She called for a line, and dialled 999.
His condition's described as stable.

Thomas Goes to the Seaside
(Health & Safety Executive Edition)

Thomas was late for the station. He was very cross with the new tilting trains, which had held him up because they could not tilt properly, and now he was running along the track, trying to make up for lost time. "Oh come along! We're rather late. Oh, come along! We're rather late," he sang to Annie and Clarabel, his two coaches. But Thomas could not seem to go faster than 100 miles an hour, no matter how hard he puffed.

"Why am I unable to exceed these silly speed restrictions?" whistled Thomas impatiently. Annie and Clarabel laughed, because the high-speed line had recently been upgraded to include Automatic Train Protection (ATP), which intervenes automatically to ensure naughty engines comply with set speed limits. "Bother! Something must be wrong with my firebox," said Thomas. By the time he got to the station, the Slim Controller was already waiting for him.

"Thomas, you are 47 minutes late, well within our performance targets for this month," said the Slim Controller, who was looking very young and fit for a man his age. "Congratulations."

"Thank you, sir," said Thomas. He noticed that the platform was crowded with schoolchildren, many of whom were shaking and crying.

"These children need to go to the seaside for the day," said the Slim Controller, "but they are afraid to ride on a train, because they think it might crash. I need you to show them how safe rail travel can be." Suddenly, much to Thomas's surprise, competent rail workers in high-visibility clothing began to uncouple Annie and Clarabel.

"Help, Thomas! Help!" shouted Clarabel.

"Where are we going?" cried Annie.

"I'm afraid that Annie and Clarabel are Mark I rolling stock," said the Slim Controller, "creaky old slam-door coaches from the 1960s. We'll be replacing them with newer stock immediately."

Thomas was sad to see Annie and Clarabel being towed away, but he was soon smiling again when he saw his two shiny new carriages, Helga and Sophie.

"We come from Sweden," they sang in lovely soft voices. As the frightened children were forced on to Thomas's two new coaches, he got a very naughty idea.

"I'll show them just how much FUN trains can be!" he peeped.

"Be a good little engine, Thomas," said the Slim Controller. "Remember that my pay incentives are directly linked to your performance." As he pulled out of the station, Thomas soon forgot the Slim Controller's warning. Instead of going directly to the seaside, Thomas headed for a main line that he knew had yet to be upgraded with ATP. Thank goodness the government had reneged on its safety commitments! Then, just as he approached the junction his brakes squealed, and poor Thomas found himself standing still on the line. "Whatever now?" he moaned.

"You passed a signal, Thomas!" sang Helga. "You passed a signal at danger!"

"Those signals are only for lazy trains who need a rest," said Thomas. "My driver passes them all the time."

"It's not up to your driver, any more, Thomas," said Sophie. "The new Automatic Warning System applies your brakes whenever you pass a signal at danger, unless your driver cancels the warning within two seconds."

"Well why didn't he, then?" demanded Thomas. "There's no one here but us!"

"Sorry," said Thomas's driver. "I'm really stoned." Slowly the train began to reverse up the tracks.

"Not to worry mate," peeped Thomas with a cheeky wink, "your secret's safe with me."

"Nothing personal," said the driver, "but it really freaks me out when you talk."

Now Thomas and Helga and Sophie were heading for the seaside once again. However, Thomas was planning more tricks to frighten his passengers. Perhaps he would derail into a field with an angry bull in it! That would teach those children not to ride on trains! Thomas looked for some faulty points, or a nice pile of wet leaves, but there were none to be found. He hoped he might spot some vandals damaging the track, but all along the way on both sides appropriate fencing had been installed to inhibit access. "It is estimated that 55 per cent of all train incidents are due to vandalism!" sang Clarabell.

"Huh," said the driver.

At the next station some policemen came and escorted Thomas's driver off the train. "We are taking you for drug testing," said one of them. "Allegations have been made under the new Confidential Incident Reporting and Analysis System – the whistleblower's charter, if you like."

"The system is open to all Railway Group members, as well as other participating companies," sang Helga and Sophie.

"Bye-bye! Good luck. Bye-bye! Good luck," puffed Thomas.

"Does anyone hear them besides me?" asked the driver.

Eventually a new driver was found for Thomas, one who had tested negative for cannabis and positive for literacy. Soon he and Helga and Sophie were under way again. Now the children were smiling as Thomas adhered strictly to prevailing speed restrictions all the way to the seaside. In the village he met Bertie Bus driving down the stretch of road that runs alongside the railway.

"Hullo, Thomas!" said Bertie. "Care to race?"

"I can't," moaned Thomas. "The track won't let me! It's called safety."

"Why, rail travel is already much safer than going by bus," said Bertie, slamming into a bridge abutment, killing four.

"Really?" said Thomas. He began to think that safety wasn't so bad after all. When he finally pulled into the station, the Slim Controller was there, waiting for him.

"How did you get here so fast?" asked Thomas.

"I flew on easyJet," said the Slim Controller. "It's very convenient, and I wanted to be here in order to give you this award for

Effective Risk Management. Thomas, you really are a safe little engine." The children cheered as they disembarked.

"Thank you," said Thomas proudly. "It remains my number-one priority."

Health by Stealth

FlipSide Solutions PR – Memo

To: All

Re: update on gov't anti-obesity promotions

As you all know, we have been charged with putting together an advertising package for the government's big anti-obesity campaign, imitating the stealth promotion and celebrity endorsements favoured by the crap food lobby. Here's where we are so far:

- **Weight Loss with Kate Moss** Fantastic idea for a blog written by supermodel Kate Moss, detailing the regime she uses to avoid obesity. The focus groups loved it, and the costings look very good. The only problem is the regime itself, but we were always going to edit – eg "carrot" instead of "cigarette" and "walking to work" replacing that stuff about chewing an entire leg of lamb and spitting it into a bin liner. Make sure Tessa Jowell doesn't see the first draft.

- **Real Fruit for Real Kids** Simple but brilliant: we get a celebrity to endorse fruit the way Beckham pushes Pepsi, with the government and the relevant growers' associations splitting the tab. It's vital we get someone with a lot of "street cred" who can make eating pears seem totally radical. So far we've had confirmation from triple-jumper Jonathan Edwards and Des O'Connor. We tried to get Liam Gallagher, but it turns out he hasn't eaten any fruit in over a decade.

- **Rave-O-Cise** Leaflets designed to look like invites to illegal parties or raves are handed out at places where young people congregate. When the "partygoers" arrive at the trendy warehouse venue, they'll have to climb 12 flights of stairs before attending what turns out to be a public debate on PFI. Kills two birds with one stone, but we'll need to go out of house for the designs. The dummies from HM Stationery Office do not look good.

Welcome to the NewsRoom at permachat.co.uk, the UK's premier online current affairs forum!

>connecting to server...

Current Host: Chris2

Current Topic: 10 more hospitals were granted foundation status this week, but England's foremost orthopaedic hospital was denied independence, amid fears that it would not be viable under the new scheme. Is the Prime Minister's mission to make all hospitals foundation hospitals within four years realistic? Is this the way to save the NHS? What do you think?

jenni@boughtledger: GO TIM

Pashmina: give it up jenni@

jenni@boughtledger: NEVER

capitalistpiglet: I was against the foundation scheme

Host_Chris2: but isn't the govt just trying to offer people choice?

jenni@boughtledger: GO TIM

bigladys has entered the NewsRoom

LadeezMan: he LOST

bigladys: hi

capitalistpiglet: yes! A choice between public and private!

Host_Chris2: Welcome to the NewsRoom, bigladys.

bigladys: can I smoke in here

Bronco: yes

jenni@boughtledger: GO TIM

Pashmina: no!!! wot abt passave smokin!

LadeezMan: hi bigladys. I like big ladys

Bronco: dont u mean bag ladys

LadeezMan: shut up

bigladys: it's "bi-Gladys" moron

Pashmina: please put yr fag out NOW

Host_Chris2: it's not illegal to smoke in chatrooms yet

Pashmina: it is in america

Host_Chris2: let's stick to the topic – is the NHS getting better? What sort of experiences have people had?

LadeezMan: I aint been to hospital since I got a smartie stuck in me ear

Pashmina: thats so cute! How old were u

LadeezMan: it was in april

jenni@boughtledger: I had the same MRSA as leslie ash

capitalistpiglet: my jaw clicks when I eat

Host_Chris2: I meant in terms of waiting times

Bronco: my legs itch for no reason

bigladys: I've got a lazy eye

Pashmina: I got a lazy susan

LadeezMan: sounds serious

Pashmina: I only got it 2 weeks ago

Bronco: wot u put on that then

Pashmina: ketchup & brown sauce & wotever

LadeezMan: really

Bronco: how did u get it

Pashmina: ebay

>connection to server has been terminated...

Let the Posh Do Our Boxing

While I was not exactly edified by photographs of Prince Harry braying for blood at a boxing match featuring his friend Mr Hugh van Cutsem this weekend past, the notion of extremely posh people knocking the hell out of each other instantly struck me as An Idea Whose Time Come Has. You will forgive my freeform syntax on this occasion, I hope, because it enables me to compress the expression into the acronym AIWTCH, which is intended to approximate the sound of an extremely posh person saying "Ouch!" as his nose is forcibly flattened against his face and blood spurts out both sides. In this case Mr van Cutsem defeated his opponent, described in the Daily Mail only as a "16-stone Welshman", but who is also, it turns out, a chartered surveyor.

As this very event was taking place at the Royal Lancaster Hotel in London, I was standing on a street corner in Rhayader, watching one Welshman knock the hell out of another, a spectacle so unedifying that I was moved to cross the road and intervene, although in the end my feet declined to participate and I remained rooted to the spot. None of the other passersby even stopped to watch, which made my interest all the more perverse.

A staged match between two aristocrats, however, is not only uncommon but a neat inversion of boxing's insalubrious roots, when large, working-class men were drafted in to beat each other up for the entertainment of the Prince Regent. I envisage the annual AIWTCH Festival as a huge, free outdoor event, with an intra-royal family bout at the top of the card. Such an event will unite Britain in a way few sports can, with a spirit pitched somewhere between a coronation and a public hanging. It won't be expressly ideological – people can root for whoever they want – but only blue blood will be spilled. If there's a downside to this, I can't see it.

Boxing has been deemed politically incorrect in recent years for many reasons, almost all of which are negated by this arrangement. No one will be exploited. Brain damage simply isn't going to be an issue. As a source of bloodstock, the aristocracy has the twin advantages of being both endangered and utterly expendable. And as most of the participants will be hunt supporters, posh-boxing is a blood sport even animal rights activists can enjoy. This is bear-baiting without the tears.

If the event at the Royal Lancaster only got it half right – the audience were, by and large, even posher than the contenders – Harry did at least look keen to have a go himself. He was reportedly so caught up in the excitement that he began shadow-boxing at ringside. How deeply endearing he can be when he tries. Once the AIWTCH Festival is up and running, Harry could well become our first pugilist prince since the Earl of Wessex's fleeting acquaintance with the sport during his all-too-brief stint with the Royal Marines, which earned him a black eye and a bloody nose. How much would you pay for a DVD of that?

I Did It Their Way

The life coach entered the public consciousness some years ago, as just another human accessory for people with more money than friends, alongside the personal trainer, the PA, the psychic and the nutritionist. If the average person encountered one, it was probably on TV, where life coaches can be found telling people to make bereavement sculptures, or to throw away all their stuff. The very term "life coach" seemed designed to convince sceptics that the discipline was nonsense. In Lucy Kellaway's satirical novel Who Moved My BlackBerry, the protagonist, Martin Lukes, a marketing executive, is in regular email contact with his life coach, Pandora, who takes the Rogerian notion of "unconditional positive regard" for her client to absurd levels: "I, your number-one fan, sincerely believe you can beat your best by 50% by year end. What is stopping you? Strive and thrive!"

Then, at the end of August, it was reported that the health secretary, Patricia Hewitt, and her civil servants were receiving life coaching. It transpired that other government departments, including No 10, the Foreign Office, the Cabinet Office and the Treasury, regularly employed life coaches at the taxpayers' expense. I still don't know what a life coach is, exactly, but if someone with as much priggish self-belief as Hewitt needs one, then I probably need two. But how do you find a life coach? Where does one start?

"You can start anywhere that makes sense," says the life coach Dr Sally Ann Law. "Either with a little bit of background about who you are and what's been going on in your life ..."

I am sitting in Law's bright attic office at her home in Crouch End. I chose her because she has a really nice website – elegant, understated, informative – although I can't quite pretend that I am just here for life coaching: even if I had managed to conceal my notepad and tape recorder, she would have eventually spotted the photographer and his equipment. If I frame my questions just so, however, it may be possible to steal a bit of free coaching while I'm here.

Law is, I think, the sort of life coach I would choose: she seems calm and utterly trustworthy. She has a reassuring manner and a PhD in psychology. I'm sure she would never tell me to throw all my possessions into a skip.

She also harbours a degree of scepticism towards the profession that rivals mine. Her website takes pains to point out that hers is a wholly unregulated field, that training schools are subject to no single accrediting body, and that basically anyone can claim to be a life coach. She doesn't even much like the title. "When I first set up my website, I tried to think of a different term," she says. "And I thought, well, I'd be mad, if people are putting 'life coach' into Google, and I'm trying to be so precious and different, and they never find me."

Luckily, she comes very near the top of the 28.5m hits one gets on typing "life coaching" into Google. There are an estimated

80,000 to 100,000 life coaches working in the UK, and probably almost as many different explanations of what exactly a life coach is. Law describes life coaching as a form of help for people who, though otherwise mentally well, "are either struggling with something specific – career, relationships or something like that – or just have a diffuse sense of, 'Why am I not happier?'"

In its faintly obscure origins, life coaching owes at least as much to management consultancy as it does to therapy. It combines the terminology and style of executive "mentoring" (a combination of managerial training and career counselling) with elements of humanistic psychology and the populist get-out-of-your-own-way mentality of such personal development gurus as Anthony Robbins. How these disparate strands are woven together depends largely on the personal tastes of the life coach in question. For its adherents, life coaching is a logical evolution in the science of mental wellbeing in a world where psychology has become highly medicalised, and where financial imperatives favour pharmacological solutions. For its detractors, life coaching is either unlicensed psychotherapy or an expensive way to have a nice chat.

"It isn't therapy, and it isn't talking to your best friend – the way I see it, anyway," says Law. "To me, life coaching is helping people work through issues that are bothering them, that they keep getting stuck in their own heads with, and trying to help them get a bit of clarity, sort out what's noise in the equation and what's really important."

While most life coaches operate solely over the phone, or even by email, Law prefers to see her clients in person, one to one, in Crouch End. She doesn't insist on long-term goals – "If you're paying attention to who you are as a person, then you're going to design the right life for yourself" – and she doesn't give homework. "I'm not going to send you away with tasks to build your confidence. You're not going to have to take something back to Woolworths to see if you can bear to talk to the sales assistant."

My other life coach, Chris, does give homework. His website is also impressive, and sprinkled with inspirational quotes such as "Fear is that little darkroom where negatives are developed". His "Living on Purpose" course – at £50, the cheapest he offers – is conducted entirely by email. Chris could, for all I knew, be a bit of computer software, although I had to dismiss this theory after he rang me up when my credit card payment failed to clear.

If I complete the course, I will receive a short sentence that gives my reason for being on earth, something like "I show the way" or "I explore in wonder". My current one, "Pay off the mortgage and die", is not even listed in the examples on the website, so I'm hopeful. After a day or so my first exercise arrives. I am to compile a list of my positive qualities, headed "My Qualities". This vaguely reminds me of the sort of primary school assignment that would have caused me to burst into tears. The answers must subscribe to the format "I am [quality]", which I find very constraining. I can't put "I am play the guitar a bit". I ignore the exercise for a week.

Although the concept of life coaching may be 20 years old in America, the industry has expanded exponentially over here in recent years, for reasons that are hard to pinpoint. "I think the availability is creating its own demand in a way," says Law. "People read about it in magazines and think, 'Well, I better go to see one.'" Also, she says, people move around a lot these days, and find themselves removed from their normal family network, operating in a social milieu where burdening your friends with your problems is considered impolite. Many of her clients are from other countries and have come to the UK for work reasons. "They're grappling with issues of, 'Shall I stay, shall I go, where's home, what's real?'"

For other people, she says, a happy outcome might mean "daring to write a book, or become a dancer, or go to drama school, buy a house in London ... decide to leave a relationship, or decide to stay in a relationship, but work out ways to do it differently". Some people come for career advice and end up addressing other issues. "And some people say I don't really know why I'm here, but I Googled life coaching and a lot of the things you said on your website speak to me." How strange, I think. Then I remember that's how I ended up here.

My first email exercise for Chris proves to be as excruciating as I had expected. After several hours, I've only got three qualities listed: "I am patient", "I am intelligent" and "I am modest", and I've spent most of my time fiddling around with the order. I am allowed to seek the help of family and friends, but consulting my wife proves to be a mistake. "Let's see," she says. "Compassionate? No. Helpful? No. Sympathetic? No. Engaging? No. Brave? No ... "

Eventually I manage 20 adjectives I can live with. I mail them off to Chris. Exercise two arrives in my inbox within 24 hours. I am to solicit a similar list of my qualities from several friends. I begin to wonder if I really want to know my life's purpose that badly.

If finding a purpose is the aim of life coaching, for an increasingly large number of people, going to see a life coach ends with the decision to become a life coach. It's easy to see why. Most coaches have themselves come to their calling after reaching some personal or professional crossroads. Law found herself promoted away from the bit of her job she liked best: interviewing people. Chris, according to his website, spent 17 years in corporate management before finding his true purpose. For those who are trying to figure out what to do with the rest of their lives, life coaches aren't just facilitators; they are templates. Templates who get up to £200 an hour. As Law says: "I work for myself. I can set my own hours, work around the kids."

The Coaching Academy – top of the Google list – offers a one-day introductory seminar, which travels around the country, for £49. "To call yourself a life coach, you would need to do our diploma course," says the woman on the end of their Freephone number. The course, she tells me, will take between six and eight months, with virtually all the coursework (about one evening a week's worth) done at home, and will cost me £2,497 + VAT. There is an optional "intense sales and marketing weekend course" to help new life coaches set themselves up in business (an additional £497). The Coaching Academy is, she says, "the most highly accredited in Europe". My e-coach, Chris, studied with them, and he sits on their executive council.

Law does not train other life coaches, but, she says: "Some people have none the less insisted that they come and be trained, so there have been four or five people who have come for sessions who want to be life coaches, and I've made it clear that I won't give them a certificate." She remains suspicious of courses that offer life-coaching qualifications (although she herself trained with a life coach called Charles Bentley, who has a very impressive website), "given that anyone can call themselves a life coach right now, and that same person can say, 'by the way, I not only coach, but I train.' That's exactly what people are doing".

Law does not, however, wish to condemn life coaches who work differently from her. "I don't think the majority of life coaches are charlatans," she says, although she admits that those trying to find a good life coach are more or less on their own. "They know, if they do any research at all, that it's an unregulated field, and if they're choosing that person, then very possibly that is the right person for them. It's OK that there are life coaches doing it other ways."

I finally send Chris a lame version of exercise two, and confess how difficult I found it all. "Yes, this is real work, isn't it?" he answers. This is swiftly followed by exercise three: a list of memories following the format, "I was fulfilled and happy when I ..." I stare at the screen. No examples spring to mind. He wants at least 10, preferably 20. At this point I think it would be easier simply to declare myself a life coach, set up a website, and be done with it. I also do training, by the way.

Flying – It Just Gets Worse

Man, do I hate flying. I hate it more each time I do it. I'll admit I've reached an age where I hate everything more each time I do it, but in this case I'm certain that the airlines are making flying worse on purpose.

I'm not what you'd call a frequent flyer, so the accumulation of fresh degradations is always a shock. It begins at the airport, where they've positioned a man near check-in to hand me a typewritten apology for the myriad inconveniences I'm about to experience thanks to new security procedures, the first of which is apparently this stupid letter. Do I look like I have a free hand?

It is, however, the plane itself that seems to have been recon-figured as an instrument of mass torture. I had been naive enough to assume that in the time since I'd last flown, the huge increase in size of the average passenger would have forced the airlines to make radical modifications. How could they do otherwise? It's not like global warming. You can't just deny people are getting fatter.

But no. The other day I got on a new plane, less than three years in service, and if anything, they've allocated less space per human. They've clearly commandeered some additional acreage from economy in order to offer in-flight tennis lessons to business flyers. When the person in front of me (a person of considerable weight, but nothing out of the ordinary) sits down, the little TV screen in the seat back bounces around alarmingly. I instantly develop a new phobia about the seat in front collapsing and killing me. I wonder if the collapse of one seat could have a domino effect, shearing chairs off their bolts all the way to the back of the plane until each passenger is lying flat on the one behind. I consider ringing for a member of the cabin crew, but in the end I decide it's best not to say anything. It will only give them ideas.

The pilot crackles on to run through the usual list of reasons why we won't be leaving just yet: baggage not loaded, fuel not quite topped up, no one around to tow us off the gate anyway, I'll let you know just as soon as we've missed our slot. Hmmm. At check-in they'd insisted I head straight to the gate, even implying that I should jog part of the way, giving me the distinct impression that we were all in a bit of a hurry. If you fly more than I do you will already know that they now incorporate all this messing around on the ground into the flight time on your itinerary, moving everything an hour further away.

Some time after takeoff, the person in front decides, not unreasonably from his point of view, to recline his seat, and the film I am watching actually touches my nose. Then a stewardess hand me a packet of Worcestershire-sauce-flavoured pretzels. Are they trying to get me to go berserk? Do they want to me to jump up and switch the doors to manual?

I notice many of the passengers now drug themselves up and put on the eye shades provided. They've created a new class since I last flew: first, business and rendition.

PermaBlog – Non-stop comment for a non-stop planet!

Are Dyslexics Just Clinically Thick?

Britain's powerful "dyslexia industry" has succeeded grouping all manner of learning difficulties under the banner of a single and highly controversial "disorder", leaving parents with the dangerous delusion that their child's lack of motivation or academic progress is the result of a condition which ... *[read more]*
Posted by MaxPersons at 0844 today

SUSPICIOUS PACKAGES AND EXTENDABLE ARMS

Max Persons is the acting deputy director of the Society of Public Policy Institutions Network Research Foundation.

COMMENTS

I don't pretend to know much about dyslexia, but there's a big difference between saying it's over-diagnosed and saying it doesn't exist.
SixKindsOfChris at 0908 today

Can I just say that I think "Are Dyslexics Just Clinically Thick?" is about the most grossly offensive headline I've ever seen on this site
JaneT at 0933 today

Worse than "Tony Blair Should Be Crucified"?
ElSmell at 0956 today

OK, maybe not, but I wasn't really around during Easter week.
JaneT at 1008 today

Chris, I take your point. JaneT, I agree: the headline is reductive and offensive, but I didn't write it
MaxPersons at 1021 today

Well I'd like to know who writes those things, then
JaneT at 1039 today

I usually write them but I got sacked this morning
conal@permablog.co.uk at 1101 today

I'm not surprised, conal
JaneT at 1110 today

I didnt get sacked for that one though, I got sacked for "Dyslexia Is Just A Hard Way To Spell Stupid". And I misspelled dyslexia when I put it up. It was helariouos
conal@permablog.co.uk at 1101 today

I'm like a dyslexic, but with laundry. Always mixing whites with colours!
Daisy88 at 1122 today

The opposite of what everyone's saying is true: dyslexia is a serious and specific condition which is often missed by teachers and GPs.
LauraW at 1128 today

Sorry to hear you got the sack conal
ElSmell at 1135 today

LauraW I think your point is well made – the dangers of not recognising the problem are far greater than this conspiracy theory about a "Dyslexia myth"
SixKindsOfChris at 1153 today

who cares pay was shite & hours terrilble, i dont want to work at no stupid bolg site full of asrewipes anywayy
conal@permablog.co.uk at 1204 today

My Jemima caught dyslexia from the MMR, but I had to go to 12 different specialists before I finally got the diagnosis I wanted.
LauraW at 1219 today

Girls cant get dyselxia
conal@permablog.co.uk at 1232 today

They can when it comes to laundry. and maps!
Daisy88 at 1236 today

You're thinking about haemophilia, conal
ElSmell at 1247 today

It's important these issues are debated rationally and in the open, and I'm glad to see it happening here
MaxPersons at 1301 today

No im not! i have a grilfreind!!!
conal@permablog.co.uk at 1312 today

---

conal, did you ever think that you might be a bit dyslexic? You seem to have trouble with your spelling
JaneT at 1320 today

To think I missed Cash in the Attic for this
SixKindsOfChris at 1329 today

Thats becos im completly wasted
conal@permablog.co.uk at 1342 today

You must be registered to post a comment

Manners & Modern Life

The Networking Queen

"Tim arrives rather late and is introduced to the others, but he's forgotten his guest list and is muddled about who's who." This is just a hypothetical scenario showing how not to behave at a business lunch, from Carole Stone's book Networking: The Art of Making Friends, but I recognised more than my name in this narrative shard. What follows is the story of my social life writ small: "Tim is horrified to realise he will be expected to say something … Ken asks Tim what he wants to say. Tim lamely repeats a point that has already been made … Tim, realising he has not made a success of the lunch, sees his chance to escape. While Ken is busy talking to someone else, Tim leaves without saying goodbye to him … In his anxiety he has also had three glasses of wine and feels muddle-headed … " I think Stone must have been at that Private Eye thing I went to a few years back, watching me and taking notes. If so, it was nice of her to say it was only three glasses.

If Stone is London's networking queen, then I am the anti-Stone. Her philosophy is: no matter the situation, always be ready to make a friend. My philosophy is: you can always run away. Stone has a database with 14,000 names in it. I have a two-page list of phone numbers torn from my 1997 diary to save me having to copy them into my 1998 diary. In the end I never bought a 1998 diary. Stone hobnobs with the great and the good. I try to stay out of the way of such people. I am the best possible test of Stone's networking primer. If she can fix me, she can fix anyone.

My first networking experience was to be Stone's book launch, held in the Covent Garden branch of Waterstone's. I had only just begun reading the book, so I had gathered few tips apart from the absolute necessity of remembering to bring business cards, which threw me into a panic. I didn't have any business cards; I've never had a business card, or indeed anyone to give one to. I spent the entire afternoon making some on my computer. They looked all right, but I wasn't sure what they should say. I didn't want to put "freelance journalist" because it makes me sound like an unsuccessful freelance journalist. I couldn't put "successful freelance journalist" because it's too long, and not strictly accurate. I toyed with the idea of simply writing "I made this card" on them, but in the end I went with "Tim Dowling, writer" and printed out a dozen.

I emerged from Leicester Square tube station at precisely 6.45pm, in a dark suit and a green power tie. The launch started at 6.30pm and I calculated that 6.55pm would be the perfect moment to arrive. I was wrong. Stone's friends are a surprisingly punctual lot, and when I got there the place was already packed, with everyone at the back straining to catch the last few words of Stone's speech. When she stood down to rapturous applause, the crowd dissolved into a fluid networking entity, a seamless weave of conversation studded with the faces of Robert Kilroy-Silk, Esther Rantzen and the astrologer Russell

Grant. There were also business leaders, journalists and non-specific rich people. I spotted Stone at the back, signing books and chatting to a few of her 14,000 mates. I knew not one soul.

I have my own tactics for dealing with such events, none of which figure in Stone's philosophy. I weaved purposefully through the crowd in a lazy figure eight, with a look on my face as if I was heading somewhere important in a hurry. I awarded myself a fresh glass of wine for each completed circuit, to calm the thudding of my heart. On my third figure eight a woman blocked my path and stuck out her hand, saying: "You're no better at this than I am! At a party like this we really should be networking!" We both laughed. Oh, how we laughed. Suddenly, two more women approached. It transpired that they knew my new friend, and I was introduced to them. They both worked for the Hungarian Cultural Centre, so we all talked about Hungary. I told them I had never been to Hungary, and they made me promise I would go. One of the women gave me her card, and I gave each of them one of mine. "Look, I made these!" I said, draining my third glass of wine. Then they all went away, and I was on my own again.

I continued my circuiting until I was stopped by another woman, who said: "I see you're not very good at this either!" She worked at Buckingham Palace, and was also trying to learn how to network. She gave me her card, I gave her mine, and we talked about how useless we were for the most of the evening. By the time she went home I had worked up the courage to introduce myself to Stone, who was rather more happy to see me than I was prepared for. She introduced me to several people in quick succession, but by this time the party was already breaking up. Right at the end I met someone I knew, who said my homemade cards were stupid.

At home I tried to follow Stone's debriefing routine, making notes about who I'd met and what had been said. I counted the cards I'd received (two) and the number I'd given away (four). I tried to recall the conversations I'd had, as well any promises I might have made, but I couldn't. Then I remembered: I had promised to go to Hungary.

A week later, fully swotted-up on Networking: The Art of Making Friends, I went along to the monthly salon that Stone holds in her Covent Garden flat, a two-hour networking frenzy for regulars and newcomers. I watched from across the road for a while as people went in, catching the occasional glimpse of the heaving networking circus behind her first-floor windows. Finally I followed someone else up the stairs to the flat, where Stone's husband, Richard, smiled as though he knew me, and gave me a glass of wine. I inched my way into the crowd and tapped Stone on the shoulder. Again I was unprepared for her enthusiasm. I'd forgotten how close we were.

Fortunately for me, networking round at Stone's is like going to a dance and having someone else move your legs for you. She took me by the arm and inserted me into a group of people, rattling off their names and professions. Among them were a surgeon and a woman who sold foreign currency. My face burned. I couldn't follow the conversation. Richard appeared from nowhere and refilled my wine glass. Stone took away the surgeon and brought us a composer instead. Then she took me away and put me into a new group with some Reader's Digest people. Stone brought more and more people into this group until it became absurdly large. Then it split into two groups and I found myself talking to the documentary-maker Roger Graef and the currency woman from the first group. Richard appeared and filled my glass. We edged toward the wall trying to keep our group intact, but Stone caught me and said: "Come and meet Lorraine Heggessey, the controller of BBC1." In Heggessey's group I met another composer. I asked him which pianos he thought were good. Richard filled my glass. At 8.30pm the party came to an abrupt end. I bid goodbye to Heggessey and headed off into the night. I tried to debrief in the taxi, but in his anxiety Tim had had too much wine and felt muddle-headed.

The next morning I found a business card in my pocket from a man who had promised to help me with my networking. Following Stone's advice to "take responsibility for the follow-up", I dithered for several days before emailing him. In the meantime, I accepted two more party invitations, to a charity auction and a magazine launch. The auction was hosted by Emma Thompson, and when I arrived I spotted her chatting to none other than my dear friend Stone. By the time I got to Stone she was no longer talking to Thompson, but she introduced me to one of the organisers and asked me if I wanted any more scalps. Then she went off to another party. I stayed behind and became muddle-headed, to the extent that I bid £120 for a T-shirt signed by Ali G. He's not even a real person. Luckily, someone else wanted it more.

The following day the man from Stone's salon rang me and offered up a networking event at the Wellcome Building, a monthly gathering called BioWednesday. He wasn't going himself, but I felt sure I could handle it on my own. It happened to be the same night as the magazine launch, so I could flit from one networking opportunity to another, just like Stone. I accepted. An email with details followed forthwith.

At six o'clock sharp I entered the Wellcome Building, my suit now showing obvious signs of wear. I collected my badge, some bumf and a glass of wine, and stood in a corner looking over the guest list. They all appeared to be leading experts in the field of biotechnology. At the bottom of the list it said "Tim Dowling", with nothing next to my name. A man sidled up to me, stuck out his hand and said: "I see you're no good at this either!" I introduced myself and asked him what biotechnology was. I didn't understand his answer. I gave up all hope of running into Stone.

Dr Malcolm Weir then gave an informal little talk entitled Bioinformatics and Proteomics. I like to think one can learn something from every experience, and in this case I discovered that having good biological rationale doesn't necessarily make a protein tractable to chemistry. During the questions I thought about asking one from Stone's guide to small talk, something like: "How do you know our hosts, Catalyst Biomedica?" but I decided to keep my mouth shut. The first question was about reverse transcriptase inhibitors.

There was 45 minutes of further networking scheduled after the lecture. I thought about what Stone would say: that a biotechnology professor is just a friend you haven't met yet. But Stone is open-hearted and disarming, and I am not. Tim, realising he had not made a success of the event, saw his chance to escape, and left without saying goodbye.

I had to walk to the magazine launch so I wouldn't get there too early. When I arrived I was sweating and nervous, and I instantly forgot all my training. I was meant to meet my wife there, but she was nowhere in sight. The layout of the room made a figure of eight impossible, so I skirted round the walls, desperately scanning the crowd for familiar faces. Finally I spotted someone I knew, and buttonholed her. She introduced me to someone, who introduced me to someone else. When my wife showed up I was chatting away merrily, looking for all the world like a changed man, but I knew better. I had changed very little, and like a fear-of-flying patient who is coaxed on to a 747 but gets off again minutes before takeoff, I was content to look on my failure as some kind of achievement. There and then I officially retired from networking. To celebrate I got well and truly muddle-headed. Carole: if you're reading this, call me.

Touching Royalty

When the Sun printed a photograph of Prince William groping the breast of a Brazilian student in a Bournemouth nightclub, eerily similar to a snap of Prince Harry doing the same in 2003, it illustrated a longstanding irony: while the royals are occasionally moved to reach out, they don't much like being touched themselves.

The Australian PM Paul Keating earned the nickname Lizard of Oz for daring to put his hand on the Queen in 1992. His successor, John Howard, was accused of the same thing in 2000. Tony Blair made Her Majesty visibly uncomfortable when he forced her to hold his hand on Millennium Eve, and there was a minor furore when Prince Charles met the Spice Girls at an awards ceremony in 1997 and Geri Halliwell pinched his bum.

This is, of course, just another example of the hypocrisy upon which royalty is based. So which of the royals can you touch? For the uninitiated, a primer:

- **The Queen** Do not touch under any circumstances – simply bow or curtsey. If you notice that she has some food stuck to her chin, then you should put some food in the same spot on your chin, and carry on as normal. If she has a wasp near her, you may shoo it away with the glove-on-a-pole provided by members of her household.

- **The Duke of Edinburgh** Although the rules regarding contact with the Royal Consort are much less strict, you should still avoid touching Prince Philip, because it might be one of the days when they use the wax one, and you might knock it over. If the Duke touches you in any way, just pretend it hasn't happened until you can get some kind of counselling.
- **Prince Charles** If he puts out his hand, you may shake it. Commoners and staff alike should avoid touching Charles under other circumstances, even when you are brushing his teeth for him.
- **William and Harry** If they offer a hand, you may lightly place your breast in it, but only if you are a lady. Photographers should never touch the princes, and in particular must watch out for Harry's amusing habit of waving his fists about as he leaves a nightclub, which can lead to an accidental breach of protocol. Under certain circumstances it is acceptable to clasp Harry under the arms, provided you are helping him out of the gutter and into a waiting 4x4.

Do You Have a Pot Farm Next Door?

According to the police, hundreds of Britain's homes have been transformed into secret "cannabis factories". Criminal gangs are refitting ordinary suburban residences in order to cultivate a powerful and lucrative form of cannabis known as "skunk", which is associated with depression, anxiety and being very, very high.

In an attempt to combat the problem, police are asking suburbanites to keep an eye out for pot-growing neighbours. But how can you tell if next door has been transformed into a skunk farm? Keep your eyes open, your curtains twitching and ask yourself the following:

- Is there a pungent smell emerging from the property? Be warned: there are many different types of pungent smell. Your neighbour might be making boutique cheeses, or running an illegal dry-cleaning service. If you're not sure what pot smells like, buy some.

- Do your neighbours mostly keep themselves to themselves, only dropping by every few months in the dead of night to borrow several hundred bin liners?

- Are their windows completely blacked out 24 hours a day, revealing only the occasional sliver of brilliant white light? Does rain sizzle and boil away when it strikes their roof? (Successful pot cultivation requires strong artificial lighting.) Then again, they might just be shooting a Woody Allen film. Call the police anyway. You might get to meet Woody Allen!

- Have you ever been inside the house? Try knocking on the door. Just say you popped by to return the extension lead which you found plugged in next to your toaster and running out the cat flap. Do your neighbours seem to be keeping an awful lot of poinsettia plants for this time of year? Do their floors suffer from a build-up of dirt exceeding a depth of six inches?

- Do they have lots of gardening equipment in their garden, even though their garden is unkempt and full of weeds? Of course, you might have lots of gardening equipment of your own, and your garden might be equally untended. Best to get out there and spruce things up, before your neighbours get suspicious and ring the police. And get rid of any giant cannabis plants you have hanging around.

The Latecomer's Handbook

Britain, you may or may not have noticed, is running behind schedule – about a day and a half late a year. On average, it's said, we now leave colleagues and friends waiting for 47.2 minutes a week, although this statistic was obtained by surveying 2,000 people in the street, people whose willingness to stop and answer questions posed by a stranger with a clipboard shows a certain lax attitude to appointment-keeping.

The main reason posited for this creeping lateness is the advent of the mobile phone. As long as we can ring up to apologise, the extra tardiness is tolerated. But with new technology comes new etiquette: just how late is it now acceptable – even advisable – to be? Below, a guide to correct arrival times:

- **Two hours early or more** Ryanair flight; Ikea sale; opening of local NHS dentist; any meeting for which you might need to plant a weapon.
- **On time** Job interview; first day of new job; day after first warning for persistent lateness; day after second warning; day after first written warning; any party with free alcohol.
- **Five to 10 minutes late** One-hour session with personal trainer; lunch with obsessively punctual friend; dinner in a restaurant; scheduled meeting with underlings; appointment with anyone who has specifically asked you to be on time.
- **Fifteen to 30 minutes late** Work, as a matter of course; lunch with habitually late friend, or obsessively punctual enemy; any Virgin train departure; rendezvous at boring museum; outdoor assignation where first person to arrive will have to stand around in the rain waiting; any party with a specific start time printed on the invitation.
- **Thirty minutes to one hour late** Day-long seminar aimed at inculcating effective work habits; any rendezvous preceded by a train journey; lunch with friend who has accepted your habitual tardiness as a regrettable part of your personality; party where there might possibly be speeches; wedding of ex-girl-/boyfriend, if invited; anything the Monday after the clocks go back.
- **Two to four hours late** Guns N' Roses gig; appointment to interview Naomi Campbell; any rendezvous preceded by a Ryanair flight; home, after a night on the lash, provided you

have rung at least once to mumble incomprehensibly; wedding of ex-girl-/boyfriend, if not invited; party where you need to meet someone in order to go to another party; evening of bad theatre followed by good restaurant.

- **One day late or more** Appointment to duel; meeting certain to end with you getting the sack; anything you wish to skip, providing you can convincingly argue that you got the wrong date; start date of new fitness/dietary regime; your dooms-day cult's final AGM.

www.happybirthday.com

The world wide web is 15 years old, and is now so much a part of our lives that it's hard to remember how we coped before it arrived. Some web users will be too young to recall that if you wanted information 15 years ago, you simply had to sit in front of the television until the relevant topic was addressed. By way of celebration, I thought I might take a personal look back at the highlights of the last glorious decade and a half:

- August 1991. Sir Tim Berners-Lee posts the computer code for his world wide web on to an internet discussion group, making it publicly available for the first time.
- 1991-1995. Nothing happens.

- September 1996. I buy a modem and hook it up to my computer. For the first time in history I am able to check and see if I have any email. I do not. Undaunted, I attempt to send my first email, a letter of complaint to my new internet service provider. In the end I have to print it out and fax it to them. There is no reply.

- January 1997. I receive my first email, from a woman in Kentucky who mistakenly thinks I'm someone she went to college with. It says, "Hi! Guess what? This is my first email!!!" I do not answer it, thinking it might be one of those computer viruses. Over the next 18 months she sends me many emails: news of mutual friends, forwarded jokes, amusing magazine articles about how tough it is being a mom, an invitation to Patty's bridal shower. I feel as if I'm connected to something huge.

- September 1998. The Google search engine is launched. At last I am able to type my own name into a box and at the press of a button receive an instant assessment of how many people in the world think I am a prick.

- February 1999. I learn how to download useless software in order to gunge up my computer's works and tie up my phone line for hours. Luckily people are now able to email me to ask why I'm engaged all the time.

- August 2001. I get my first computer virus, buy a rake online and marvel at the sudden explosion in the number of people who think I am a prick.

- 2003. Broadband becomes widely available. I, along with millions of others, discover that no matter what type of activity Paris Hilton is engaged in of a Friday night, she is never too busy to answer her phone. Our innocent curiosity accidentally makes her famous.
- January 2004. I try playing poker online. Though I am very bad at it indeed, I do almost nothing else for the next six months.
- October 2004. I get wireless broadband, enabling me to keep track of how many people think I am a prick from any room in the house. Except, it transpires, my office.
- February 2005. The YouTube site is launched, marking the point at which the world wide web and I stop evolving together: I can understand why people might want to upload clips of themselves dancing to Shakira, but I don't understand why anyone else would want to see them. Never mind – I've been on the cutting edge of this technology for long enough. Let the youngsters take over.

Americans Abroad

I will confess that my first impression of Britain, after arriving from America at the age of 27, was neither poetic nor original. Looking out the taxi window, I did not at once apprehend the air of pervasive melancholy, or remark upon the begrimed splendour of London's glowering facades. I just noticed how easy it would be to amend all the TO LET signs so they read TOILET, and wondered why no one had bothered. "What is it with these people?" I thought to myself. "Have they no sense of humour?"

Americans don't travel well. We are one of our least successful exports, to the extent that the US state department, in conjunction with US businesses, has issued a 16-point pamphlet telling its citizens how to avoid behaving idiotically while abroad. It advises them not to brag and not to lecture. It says it is inappropriate to tell people about the Bible "unless you are a professional missionary identified as such".

This is a good idea. There are undoubtedly some Americans who will look at the tips and decide against travelling at all – if they can't bore on about the Superbowl or walk around Paris recommending the Bible to people, what's the point? But it doesn't go far enough for American visitors to Britain. If you want to avoid being openly hated, by all means take the state department's advice, but if you wish to escape being secretly loathed, you need to take the following extra precautions.

Don't bring along any articles about British food clipped from the travel section of your local newspaper. The information therein does not apply. People rarely eat any of those foods with quaint names – plum duff, spotted dick, etc – commonly associated with Britain. They are being laid on for your benefit, or rather as a sort of prank.

In the UK, overt displays of friendliness are taken as a sign of brain damage. This sounds horrible, but actually it's a fairly good rule of thumb. Try to match your moroseness to those around you. Occasionally you will run across that rare British person who is not just friendly but outgoing, helpful, charming and loquacious. He is a con man.

Try not to walk about dressed for several competing extremes of weather. This is an insult to the natives. You're making it look as if their country is barely habitable. Also, check to see what your clothes are advertising: is it a software firm in your home state, or a local roofing contractor, or your Bible studies group's rafting weekend? Contrary to popular belief, such T-shirts are not conversation-starters.

Finally, ask yourself: do you hate George Bush enough to travel? You may think you hate him a lot, but once abroad your denunciations of the man and his policies will have to be forthright and tireless. Every time you want to say, "So you guys say crisps for chips, and chips for fries, right?", stop, think, and then say "George Bush – what an asshole" instead. Soon people will start smiling at you on the bus. But don't take it too far: America has her spies everywhere.

PermaBlog – Non-stop comment for a non-stop planet!

Why The Blogosphere Needs A Lesson In CyberCivility
The web emerged from a kind of democratic foment: there were feuds and disputes, but the sense of a community with collective responsibility held fast. Today that community has been hijacked by abusive language, cyberbullying and vandalism. To call for certain standards of behaviour to be observed – and enforced – is hardly censorship; in fact it is essential to the very ... *[read more]*

    Posted by ShroomC at 0901 today

    Larry "Shroom" Czyzowski is an internet pioneer widely recognised as the inventor of the term "LOL".

COMMENTS

I agree that standards have slipped, not least here on PermaBlog, but I'm not sure a code of conduct can be enforced. Isn't it the job of an online community to police itself?
SixKindsOfChris at 0912 today

This is just another effort to control opinion and manufacture consent, IMHO.
ElSmell at 0919 today

I understand the concerns about censorship, but surely it wouldn't hurt if we all tried to be more polite. Hi Chris. Nice eater?

JaneT at 0927 today

What's that supposed to mean?

SixKindsOfChris at 0936 today

Dear ShroomC – can you pleeeeeease fuck off. Thanks so much.

MegaDave at 0945 today

THE RUDENESS HERE IS INVARIABLY LIBERAL IN ORIGIN. CENSORSHIP IS FINE WITH ME

SPECIALRELATIONSHIP at 0951 today

Dear MegaDave: I expected remarks like that to crop up. It only proves my point: the bulk of comment on most blogs is puerile, pointless and offensive.

ShroomC at 1001 today

And unread. Don't forget unread.

liberati at 1013 today

Sorry Chris I meant to say nice easter!!!!!! What must you think!!!!

JaneT at 1017 today

dick

MegaDave at 1018 today

ShroomC – I just looked up "LOL" on wikipedia and it doesn't say anything about you inventing it.

ElSmell at1025 today

That's because I am barred from editing that page because I called its author a turd on a new media webforum. My revenge was swift.

ShroomC at 1042 today

Sorry, JaneT. I guess the blogosphere is still prone to lots of misunderstandings. I had a lovely Easter. What did you do?

SixKindsOfChris at 1054 today

After much consideration, I decided to freeze my eggs.

JaneT at 1108 today

Hi. As a newcomer to this blog, can I just say that I am going to kill everyone on here.

badpaul at 1110 today

Good thinking, Jane. I didn't realise the weather was going to be so warm, and by the time I got to my parents, there was melted chocolate all over the back seat!

SixKindsOfChris at 1114 today

badpaul – you forgot the magic word
ElSmell at 1123 today

Shut up idoit Im coming after you right now get ready to die
badpaul at 1131 today

Yes, well, I was always the practical one. gotta go.
JaneT at 1140 today

Look badpaul, your silly threats do nothing to further the debate – why don't you put forward an argument like a real man, instead of engaging in mindless personal abuse?
ShroomC at 1146 today

I cant now my mums taking me swimming
badpaul at 1153 today

You must be registered to post a comment

A Very Merry Christmas – for Next Year

Everything about Christmas seems to be happening earlier this year. My wife's annual Christmas lecture, in which she posits an alternative holiday season where I don't ruin everything by being so unpleasant, arrived 10 days early. The traditional episode where my debit card is declined at an off-licence by someone wearing a jolly Santa hat happened right at the beginning of the month. And my yearly attack of Festive Stress, which normally strikes at 8pm sharp on Christmas Eve in a perfume counter queue, arrived three days ago.

Christmas is already the most front-loaded holiday of the year, but what used to be a month of intensive preparation has increasingly become one of premature celebration, with every party a miniature simulacrum of Christmas Day. People who go away at Christmas often have a pre-Christmas Christmas. My children are already hopped up on sugar and exhaustion. My coat pockets are full of paper hats. The TV schedules are crammed with the sort of holiday family fare that makes me glad we have two televisions. If we're going to do it this way, shouldn't we take time off work now as well and be done with it?

It was inevitable that I would snap a bit earlier this year. A chance trip to the West End in London on a non-Yule-related errand brought me into contact with Christmas shoppers a week before I was ready. I invariably weep at the school play, but this time I actually cried in the queue to get in. On Saturday evening I placed a phone call that, in retrospect, clearly constituted a cry for help. "Thank you," said the voice at the other end. "Your vote for Andy has been registered."

There I was, fresh from yet another Christmas lunch, lying

on the sitting-room floor surrounded by walnut shards, The X-Factor final blaring away, with one of my children crying over my failure to supply him with a sufficiency of AAA batteries and another holding me by the ears and shouting into my face, "You need to keep voting! Keep voting for Andy!" That's when I realised that as far as my nervous system was concerned, Christmas had already happened.

Now I'm suffering from Post-Festivity Stress Disorder, an affliction that normally sets in the day after Boxing Day and is characterised by a curious sense of detachment and an irrational fear that everyone you meet is going to hand you a glass of white wine and a mince pie. Except it's not irrational, because that's exactly what keeps happening. Every morning I wake up thinking that the whole thing is over and I can go back to work, and then it dawns on me that there are still two weeks of overeating and festive family viewing ahead.

I still can't quite shake the delusion that Christmas has been and gone, and to be honest I'm finding it rather comforting. So I just pretend that everyone is talking about next Christmas, and that it will be a good 12 months before I have to watch World's Strongest Man again. Tomorrow, in fact, I start detoxing and going to the sales.

Basic Skiing Etiquette

A Swiss resort's decision to post a 30kph speed limit on one of its runs heralds a new era in the codification of ski etiquette. The rule being enforced here – Don't Kill People – is fairly obvious, but ski etiquette has its finer points, and a basic primer, based on my own considerable experience, may be of help to the untutored.

- **No talking on the ski lift** Never feel compelled to break the awkward silence, even if the lift stops for a prolonged period. I don't care where you're from or where you're staying, and I do not want to talk about the conditions. But yes, I will have a mint, thanks.
- **Don't stand in front of the giant map** Users of public transport will find this rule familiar, but you'd be surprised how many people line their families in front of a piste map for a photograph, when some of us need to use it in order to locate the nearest Mars Bar.
- **Stick to your skill level** If you are an extremely good skier, then you and I should be nowhere near each other. Any run on which I am to be found is, by definition, too easy for you, so take your fancy technique elsewhere. You don't see me lying down in the middle of the black run on the north face, do you? Well, there was that one time I got lost. Someone was standing in front of the map.

- **Do not ask if me I'm all right when my face is caked with snow** No, I am not all right. I do not require assistance, just some privacy so that I can continue crying. Yes, that is my ski way up there. Would you? Thanks.
- **I am a human being, not a slalom gate** Even if I have stopped in the middle of the hill to adjust the angle of my hat, there is no need for you and your snowboarding friends to make tightly carved turns round me. If you are wondering how wide a berth to give me, just imagine that I am trying to hit you with one of my poles. That is what I am imagining.
- **No, I don't know how fast 30kph is either, but if I am doing anything approaching that speed you should assume that I can't stop** Technically you may have the right of way, but if I were you I wouldn't stand my ground on principle.

Friends: When to Get Rid of Them

If new survey-based evidence is to be believed, friendships among the under-30s last an average of five years or less. We all know that sometimes it is best to lose touch, but who should you ditch first, and when? Here is a handy guide to friendship shelf-life ...

- **10 years to lifetime** Neighbours who are doctors; people who possess compromising photos of you; family members; hangers-on; co-dependants; imaginary friends; low-maintenance friends; fellow monks; friends who might conceivably one day be in a position to dedicate a book to you; people with access to libellous gossip.

- **Five to 10 years** Cell mates; those changed by fame; those who can't adjust to your fame; best friends who subsequently marry your ex; schoolfriends who grow up to be stupid.

- **Two to five years** Work colleagues; drinking buddies; fellow book-club members; user-friendly school-gates acquaintances; the amusingly rude; the indiscrete; flatmates who remain unemployed for this duration; friends who side with your ex; friends whose spouses you can't stand; anyone who fails to notice that you have been carrying a torch for them all this time.

- **One to two years** Vicar, prior to child gaining place at C of E school; friends who know famous people but fail to introduce you within the allotted time frame; teens who congregate on the corner near your regular parking space; friends whose shortcomings, it transpires, closely match your own; restaurant owners; dinner party deadwood.

- **Six to eight months** Tories; sister of former boyfriend; anyone pregnant with triplets; friends-of-friends who are planning a lavish party; people who can't drive; web-based friends; anyone whose surname you can't remember after all this time.

- **One to three months** Ex-boyfriends/girlfriends who clearly don't want to give things another try; acquaintances who strike you as capable of burglary; fellow reality show contestants; upstairs neighbours.

- **Two weeks or less** Acquaintances made during a management team-building exercise; anyone you meet on holiday; anyone who appears to be able to see right through you.

- **Twenty-four hours or less** Fellow passengers in stuck lift; fellow passengers on stalled train; first colleague you speak to on first day of new job; person sitting next to you at wedding; strangers who are in a position to do you a favour but subsequently decline to help; famous people you have met when drunk; anyone, 24 hours before the Earth explodes.

Politics & Religion

Shelf Life: My Little Bible With Cuddly Puppy Gift Set

Sundays present a special dilemma for shrines. As holy places they must feel particular pressure to Keep Sunday Special, but Sunday is also a very big shopping day for them. If you build a shrine, the pilgrims will come, and they will want ice cream.

The village of Little Walsingham in Norfolk has been a place of pilgrimage since 1061, when Lady Richeldis de Faverches had her first vision of the Virgin Mary, so they've had plenty of time to sort this dilemma out. Here the church bells and the shop tills ring in harmony all Sunday long. It's a great place to pick up all manner of holy souvenirs, spiritual aids and devotional bric-a-brac. This is where I found, and subsequently purchased, the My Little Bible With Cuddly Puppy Gift Set, not because I wanted it, but because I needed some change in a hurry. In Little Walsingham the Lord's Day brings no respite from the holy obligation to Pay & Display.

The connection between the Bible and the cuddly puppy is not an immediately obvious one. The cuddly puppy is not a traditional religious icon, after all. There are no cuddly puppies in the Bible, at least not in the King James version. In fact I happen to know there are only 15 references to dogs in the whole of the KJV, three of which are to dead dogs, and two of which involve dogs returning to their own vomit for metaphorical purposes. Nothing cuddly about that. I can see no reason to package a cuddly puppy with a Bible in a gift set, except to mitigate the disappointment a child might feel at being given a bible for a present.

Taken on its own, My Little Bible In Pictures by Kenneth N Taylor is an undemanding version of God's word, with an illustration on every other page, how-well-did-you-read questions at the end of each passage ("What are these people doing? Why is this bad?") and some bowdlerised versions of Old Testament highlights: "These two women are fighting over a baby. Each says the baby is hers. God made King Solomon know which woman was really the baby's mother. He gave the baby back to its mother. Then everyone thanked God for giving them such a wise king." Scene missing, or what?

It might work better if the cuddly puppy actually appeared in some of the stories, to lead the Israelites out of Egypt, or to turn water into Ribena, or just to tell a few Bible jokes. If this happens in a future version, I have a joke to submit for consideration: Q. Why did the cuddly puppy cross the road? A. To returneth to his own vomit, as the fool returneth to his folly. Don't worry Mr Kenneth N Taylor, there's plenty more where that came from.

Welcome to the NewsRoom at www.permachat.co.uk, the UK's premier online current affairs forum!

>connecting to server...

Current Host: Chris2

Current Topic: George W Bush is here for his first state visit. Not surprisingly, protests are expected by groups objecting to the President's stance on Kyoto and his proposed Missile Defence System. Is the "special relationship" between the US and Britain now obsolete, or more important than ever? What do you think?

capitalistpiglet: r u going 2 the mooning thing in trafalgar sq?

LizFromOz: it depends? On what the weather's like? What abt u?

Pashmina has entered the NewsRoom

capitalistpiglet: I dunno. I tried to write "no 2 star wars" on my bum last night, but I got mixed up in the mirror, and now it won't come off.

Pashmina: omilord wot have I walked in on

LadeezMan: wotsit say now?

capitalistpiglet: "no 2 raw rats"

LadeezMan: its better than yes 2 raw rats

Pashmina: hello? Am I invisibile?

LadeezMan: hi pash. No 2 raw rats!

Host_Chris2: Pashmina, how will you be marking George Bush's first visit to the UK?

LizFromOz: maybe you should write it backwards on some newspaper first? And then sit in the paint?

Pashmina: its not his first visit. He woz just here!

Host_Chris2: This is Bush's first visit to Britain. Maybe you're thinking of his trip to Europe last month. Or perhaps Bill Clinton's recent appearance at Wimbledon?

Pashmina: no

capitalistpiglet: I've got to get the raw rats off first.

Pashmina: oops! I was thinkin of Michael Jackson. never mind

LadeezMan: LizFromOz, wot r u going to put on yr bum

Host_Chris2: George Bush is the president of the United States, Pashmina

LizFromOz: I've already got a tattoo there? It's like a big speech bubble with HELLO FROM DOWN UNDER in it?

Pashmina: durh! I know! dont patrotise me, Chris2

jenni@boughtledger has entered the NewsRoom

LadeezMan: nice

Host_Chris2: I apologise. Now if we could return to the topic...

jenni@boughtledger: OK PEOPLE! The final vote for the NewsRoom pub meet is in!!! AND THE WINNER IS...

LadeezMan: pash did u vote?

Pashmina: no

jenni@boughtledger: ...THE RAT & PARROT in covent garden! Wednesday 15 August!

Host_Chris2: Once again I feel I should remind everyone that the pub meet is not an official permachat event.

jenni@boughtledger: Must dash! I'll let you know about the minibus!

jenni@boughtledger has left the NewsRoom

LadeezMan: pash r u going?

Pashmina: no. u?

LadeezMan: geuss not

capitalistpiglet: I'm gonna go. What about u LizFromOz?

LizFromOz: I will absolutely, positively, definitely be there?

>connection to server has been terminated...

Seven New Deadly Sins

An Oxford University publishing project has re-evaluated the seven deadly sins and found them to be largely obsolete. The philosopher Simon Blackburn argues that lust, in particular, has been given a bad name, and should be "reclaimed for humanity".

The notion that the seven deadly sins, first catalogued in the 6th century, are incompatible with modern life is hardly shocking. Not even one of them is against the law any more. A few, such as gluttony, envy and avarice, are vital components of a healthy retail sector. New sins that reflect current morality are needed urgently. The following draft list is ready for your consideration:

1 **Biting** Why this never made the original seven is beyond me. It's a much bigger problem than pride, and most of us know from personal experience that being bitten is much worse than being envied. It's also one of the few ethical proscriptions that applies to both toddlers and pets.

2 **141** If you don't want the person you're calling to know your phone number, then don't call them. You may believe you have the moral right to withhold your number simply because BT has provided you with the facility, but this is morally specious, a bit like saying that if God hadn't wanted us to be gluttons he wouldn't have created Ben & Jerry's.

3 **Self-belief** Fully three-quarters of the trouble in the world is perpetrated by people who have every confidence that they are doing the right thing; the rest is down to freak weather. For a long time now, self-belief has actually been used as a justification for doing ill. Enough is enough: it's time we had a value system that rewards crippling self-doubt. Of course nobody wants to prevent people from believing in themselves wholeheartedly, so long as they understand they are going to hell for it.

4 **Voter apathy** 2004 only. Under the new scheme, deadly sin number 4 would be changed every 12 months to keep pace with shifting values. In 2005 it will either be poor seamanship or publishing your poetry on the internet, pending a final decision by the regulatory body.

5 **Hype** The forces of hype are in constant conflict with our

profound moral obligation not to care much one way or the other about most things.

6 Bestiality It may not be the most pressing problem facing society, but it will be a good long while before some Oxford philosopher speaks up for it.

7 Sloth This old deadly sin can stay on for the time being; I can't be bothered to come up with another.

Welcome to the NewsRoom at permachat.co.uk, the UK's premiere online current affairs forum!

>connecting to server...

Current Host: Chris2

Current Topic: The United Nations summit on racism in Durban has focused attention on Europe and America's role in the slave trade, with various delegates calling for apologies and even reparations. Should Britain apologise for slavery? What do you think?

Bronco: its the pressure of fame init

Pashmina: yes

LadeezMan: wot is

Bronco: that distroyed the marraige of Kate Wimslet & some guy

LadeezMan: never herd of her

Pashmina: she broke up with jamie theakston cos she was too famous

Bronco: thats right

Pashmina: which is wierd because he is much more famous than she is!

LadeezMan: wot a bitch

Host_Chris2: without wishing to inhibit the free flow of ideas, I feel duty bound to point out that Kate Winslet's ex is called Jim Threapleton...

LadeezMan: never herd of him niether

Host_Chris2: ...and that Jamie Theakston has just split from actress Joely Richardson

Pashmina: Go Chris2! u been reading heat or something!

LadeezMan: I never herd of any of these people

jenni@boughtledger has entered the NewsRoom

Host_Chris2: I did have a long wait at the dentist yesterday. Could I persuade anyone to address the topic?

jenni@boughtledger: yo room. Bling-bling

Pashmina: any cavities Chris2

Bronco: I thought this was the topic

jenni@boughtledger: respect to the posse. bling bling

Host_Chris2: Today's topic: should Britain apologise for its trade in slaves?

Pashmina: to who

Host_Chris2: to whom

NakedWetTracey has entered the NewsRoom

Pashmina: exactly! its to late to say sorry! They shoudnt of done slavery in the 1st place!!!

jenni@boughtledger: big up 2 the permachat massive. Bling bling

NakedWetTracey: Hi! I'm Tracey and I'm naked, ready & waiting! To see my latest pix, just click on the link www.nakedwet tracey.com/. Hope to see you there!

Bronco: I am v sorry abt slavry

NakedWetTracey: Hi! I'm Tracey and I'm naked, ready &

NakedWetTracey has been kicked out of the NewsRoom

Host_Chris2: advertising is not permitted in the NewsRoom or any other permachat site

LadeezMan left the NewsRoom

Bronco has left the NewsRoom

Pashmina: there they go

Host_Chris2: Does anyone have a final comment on slave reparations?

jenni@boughtledger: bling bling

Pashmina: who's there

>connection to server has been terminated...

The Gospel According to Jeffrey Archer

Now just you listen to me: and so it came to pass that Joseph and his extremely attractive wife Mary entered the city of David, called Bethlehem. Mary was with child at the time and in need of rest after their long journey, but none of the inns had any vacancies.

"This is ridiculous," said Joseph, consulting his special-edition Rolex. He thought of complaining but realised there was no point. Eventually one innkeeper allowed them to lodge in his filthy stables. That night Mary's child was born and laid in a manger, a sort of disgusting feeding trough. The conditions were unspeakable and unlike any you will have experienced, unless you have had the misfortune to be wrongly imprisoned for your beliefs. They named the child Jesus, which means "Jeffrey", but in those days their primitive alphabet had no F. Or Y.

Now in this same district there were shepherds out in the fields keeping watch over their flock, when an angel came unto them and said, "Listen carefully. I have information of the utmost importance. Today a deliverer has been delivered unto you. Go and seek Him. This is not a drill." And with this, the whole sky lit up like an enormous and beautiful Christmas tree.

Shortly after this extraordinary event happened, three Wise Kings, who also happened to be interested in astrology, just happened to be looking at the sky when they saw a new star rising in the constellation of Sagittarius, the Archer. "It is a sign," they said, for the Wise Kings knew that the star meant a new Messiah had been born unto them, one who would be generally interested in travelling and meeting new people, with a restless mind, but also fun to be with. "Let us go and find this Jeffrey the Archer," they said.

And so the three kings followed the star to the dirty, stinking farmyard. They came bearing expensive gifts – unlike the shepherds, who had come empty-handed – and were granted immediate access. They bowed to the ground and offered their gifts of gold and frankincense and Krug. They told Mary and Joseph of the star that had led them there, and of many things about their child that they could not have known, of His being the Son of God, the Messiah, and of His strong sense of morality and good organisational skills. "Indeed, this is a great Christmas present to the world," said Mary.

Meanwhile, an angel appeared unto Joseph and said to him, "It has come to my attention that King Herod intends to kill your special, clever Baby. Rise up and take the Child and his mother unto Egypt and don't do anything – I repeat, anything – until you hear from me." Mary quickly regained her figure and the three of them went to Egypt where they remained for a long time until the coast was clear.

By this time Jeffrey had grown big and strong and full of wiseness. Many people came to hear Him speak and they were truly impressed by His delivery. He proved to be a natural leader and above all a master storyteller, delivering unto His people The 11th Commandment ("Breathtaking … the best book I have ever read" – Amazon.com review), performed many spectacular miracles and raised millions for charity. For a time it seemed as if everyone was against Him, but that didn't bother Him in the least. He kept right on doing what He knew to be right, until eventually He was wrongly crucified for a crime He didn't commit. Undaunted, He rose again, where-upon He was seated on the right-hand side of the Lords. The parallels are incredible.

One day in the not too distant future He will come unto us again, unless of course He is already here. This is based on a true story. Amen.

Welcome to the NewsRoom at permachat.co.uk, the UK's premier online current affairs forum!

>connecting to server…

Current Host: Chris2

Current Topic: Tomorrow 10 new countries join the European Union, but what will enlargement mean in the long term for Europe as a whole, and for Britain in particular?

Pashmina: ukrania

Host_Chris2: no

Pashmina: spain

Host_Chris2: no

Pashmina: monaco

Host_Chris2: no

Pashmina: how many more I got left

Host_Chris2: you haven't got any right yet

Pashmina: majorca

Host_Chris2: no

Pashmina: slovania

Host_Chris2: I'll give you that one – Slovenia and Slovakia are joining

Pashmina: u should give me 2 then!

Host_Chris2: where is everybody?

Pashmina: bank holiday wknd innit

cymrujim has entered the NewsRoom

Host_Chris2: I suppose they've left work early

cymrujim: sut maes pashmina

Pashmina: wot

Host_Chris2: welcome to the NewsRoom, cymrujim. I'm afraid it's a bit quiet today

cymrujim: that was how are you pashmina in Welsh

Pashmina: oh I thougt u was a cypriot like my x-boyfriend

Host_Chris2: you're getting warm there. A Cypriot from where?

Pashmina: crewe

Host_Chris2: No, I mean where do most Cypriots come from?

Pashmina: london

cymrujim: I would say cyprus

Host_Chris2: exactly – and Cyprus joins the EU tomorrow. A point to cymrujim

Pashmina: you was helpin him!!

Host_Chris2: he was first with the answer

cymrujim: diolch yn fawr iawn chris2

Pashmina: his spellin aint up to much is it

cymrujim: that was thank you very much chris2 in Welsh

Pashmina: wales!

Host_Chris2: no

Pashmina: luxemberg or wotever

Host_Chris2: no. where might you find a Malteser? Or a Pole?

cymrujim: this is fun

Pashmina: on the floor of a cinema & up yr arse

cymrujim: do you speak any languages pashmina

Pashmina: I only speak pashminian

Host_Chris2: sadly no one else does

cymrujim: wow! I didn't even know there was a place called Pashmina!

Pashmina: dont worry you aint never goin there

>connection to server has been terminated...

The Super-Saints

I've always had a soft spot for St Joseph of Copertino, very much the bronze medallist in the "saints named Joseph" stakes (finishing well behind St Joseph, Dad of Jesus, and Joseph of Arimathea, alleged one-time possessor of the Holy Grail). Perhaps this is because the fact that he could fly wasn't taken into account. In fact he levitated so many times, in front of so many reputable witnesses, that he became known as the Flying Friar. Now Jesus's old man may have borne his doubts about the virgin birth with admirable stoicism – if it bothered him, he never let it affect his carpentry – but could he fly? No.

So I was pleased to hear that Joseph of Copertino has finally found his rightful place as a fully fledged comic book super-hero. The patron saint of pilots and flight attendants is to be the subject of The Flying Friar, a lightly embellished graphic novel detailing his life and exploits. It's an obvious idea when you think about it: what Celebrity Big Brother does for people who used to be famous, so the comic book industry may do for the cults surrounding some of our more obscure spiritual idols. Writers with a handy copy of the Oxford Dictionary of Saints will find themselves positively spoilt for choice.

St Rumwold, for example, was a grandson of a seventh-century Mercian king. Although he died three days after he was born, he still found time to preach a sermon on the Holy Trinity and "the need for virtuous living" before predicting his own death and then promptly fulfilling the prophecy, making him the ideal patron saint for people with short attention spans. If you gave him a way with mordant one-liners and a cigar, and maybe laser eyes, he'd be a perfect superhero for our times.

St Winefride, the Welsh virgin, had her head cut off by a prince whose offer of marriage she refused, but that didn't stop her getting a job as the abbess of a nunnery at Holywell. It took more than a little decapitation to stop Winefride. "This is turning out to be one hell of a morning," she says to the dumbstruck prince as she grabs her own head by the hair in what film critics will almost certainly describe as the CGI sequence of 2008.

St Egwin, the bishop of Worcester, locked his feet in fetters and threw the key into the Avon. Then, many years later, while on a pilgrimage to Rome, he bought a fish in the market and found the key inside. It's unclear whether he was still wearing the fetters when he bought the fish, but I think for the purposes of the big-budget animated feature it works better if he is. And if he has a talking donkey friend voiced by Eddie Murphy.

And Simeon Stylites, as everybody knows, spent the last part of his life standing atop a series of tall pillars, the better placed to re-route any asteroids or comets that threatened the earth. This didn't happen in his lifetime, but would it do any harm to stick in an upper-atmosphere explosion near the end? If you ask me, a lot of these saints' lives are pretty far-fetched anyway.

Here's One We Elected Earlier

Official transcript of Blue Peter episode featuring Tony Blair, taped September 1 2006 (to be broadcast as live on D-Day minus 30).

Konnie Huq: We've got an extra-special guest with us today on the programme.

Gethin Jones: That's right, it's the prime minister, Tony Blair, who is currently on something called a "legacy tour" of the United Kingdom.

KH: Welcome to Blue Peter, prime minister.

Tony Blair: Thank you. It's very nice to be here.

GJ: I wonder if you could just explain to us what your legacy tour is all about.

TB: It's basically, well it's a way of, let's say, underscoring the triumphs of New Labour, and of capitalising on our achievements, especially in the realm of ideas.

KH: And this is all because soon Britain will be getting a brand-new prime minister.

TB: Hmm.

GJ: And when will the change take place?

TB: You know, I think I've said all I have to say on that, Gethin.

KH: It's June, isn't it? That's what I heard.

TB: Whatever happens, there will be plenty of time for a stable and orderly transition, I've said all that. Frankly I don't think your viewers are too terribly interested in this sort of …

GJ: We've got an email here from Daisy from Tenbury Wells in

Herefordshire, who's 10, and she says: "Dear Tony Blair, please can you tell me exactly when you are going to step down?"

TB: Well, I'd like to know who put her up to that.

KH: So you won't say when you're going to step down?

TB: No. I'm not even going to say when I'm going to say when I'm going to step down.

GJ: During your leadership we've heard a lot about something called Blairism. Can you just tell us a bit about what Blairism means?

TB: I suppose it's about changing the political landscape, you know, winning the battle of ideas. Reforming public services, a strong economy, trying to make things better for ordinary people.

KH: But it's also about war, isn't it?

TB: I thought we were supposed to be making biscuits or something.

KH: Because you started a war.

TB: I mean, I don't know why you asked for the flapjack recipe in the first place, if you weren't …

GJ: And lots of people supported the idea of going to war in Iraq.

TB: They did, yes. I think they understood the …

GJ: But many, many more people didn't.

TB: I don't know where you're getting your figures from, frankly.

KH: And some of the intelligence you put forward to make the case for going to war turned out not to be true, didn't it?

TB: I'm sorry, but what happened to the flapjack segment? Where are the ones we made earlier?

KH: Are you afraid that the legacy of the war – the ongoing chaos in Iraq, not to mention the wholesale destabilisation of the Middle East and the alienation of large sections of Britain's Muslim population – will overshadow your successes with, say, PFI and Lords reform?

TB: That's a very big question.

KH: It comes from Keiran in Sleaford near Lincoln.

TB: Well, Keiran, I've been travelling all round Britain recently; been to Scotland and Wales, been on Songs of Praise and Chris Evans, going to the Eden project next week, might join the Arctics on stage at Glastonbury, that's still up in the air …

KH: Could you answer Keiran's question, please? He's eight and has to wear a leg brace.

TB: Listen, it's not just … Oh, look! Hello, Shep! Good boy. Come here. How are you?

KH: That's Meg.

GJ: Shep's dead, sir. Shep's dead.

TB: (Awkward silence) Look, it's, uh, been great coming on to talk to you, but I'm taping with Sharon Osborne in half an hour, so …

GJ: Before you go we would just like to give something in honour of your time as prime minister.

TB: Steady on! I haven't quit just yet.

KU: As well as something for the whole Blair family. Six Blue Peter badges!

TB: Well, that's very nice, thank you, but I'm afraid we don't really have the space to look after animals properly. Wouldn't they be better off in a zoo?

PermaBlog – Non-stop comment for a non-stop planet!

A Cross to Bear

When the prime minister said that "there are some battles really, really not worth fighting" in relation to the British Airways "cross at work" row, he effectively defended the triumph of political expediency over ideology. Without condemning or supporting BA's policy, he simply ... *[read more]*

Posted by Max Persons at 0845 today

Max Persons is acting deputy director of the Society of Public Policy Institutions Network Research Foundation.

COMMENTS

At my work they give a written warning just for wearing an "I Love Santa" T-shirt

MegaDave at 0929 today

Down with Christmas killjoys!
JaneT at 0935 today

Sorry that should say "I Love Satan". Hard to type with these gloves on
MegaDave at 0941 today

IT'S JUST ANOTHER FORM OF RELIGIOUS INTOLER-ANCE
SPECIAL RELATIONSHIP at 0958 today

That's exactly what I said. They even made me take out my tongue spike because people couldn't understand me on the phone
MegaDave at 1011 today

Blair is right. The correct answer to this conflict is "who cares"
liberati at 1016 today

How can you say that liberati! What about someone's right to express their faith?
JaneT at 1019 today

What about BA's right to enforce a dress code, which is identical to police force and army policy?
SixKindsOfChris at 1025 today

"who cares"

liberati at 1031 today

THE SIKHS ARE ALLOWED TO WEAR THEIR SYMBOLS

SPECIAL RELATIONSHIP at 1040 today

Your talking about apparel which is required by their religion.

SixKindsOfChris at 1047 today

You can't have one rule for one religion and another rule for another!

JaneT at 1049 today

Then they made me wear a stupid badge that said "It's My Pleasure To Serve You." And when I crossed out "You" and wrote in "The Dark Lord" they were all like, second written warning!

MegaDave at 1102 today

---

driver not let me take light saber on bus. I tell I am jedi!

SE14 at 1107 today

Where do you draw the line? It's an interesting point.

JaneT at 1117 today

No overt symbols in the workplace, full stop.

SixKindsOfChris at 1121 today

I told the supervisor that what I did with my foreskin was my own business, but he was like "when the chain's attached to your ear at the other end, then it becomes my business".
MegaDave at 1138 today

AND YOU WONDER WHY YOU DON'T HAVE A JOB MEGA-DAVE
SPECIAL RELATIONSHIP at 1139 today

Chris are you saying I shouldn't be allowed to have a tiny cross nestling in my cleavage?
JaneT at 1142 today

What are you talking about? I'm at work right now.
MegaDave at 1144 today

It's fine as long as it's not where everyone can see it
SixKindsOfChris at 1146 today

Got to go, people. Some dickhead wants me to sell him a printer.
MegaDave at 1146 today

No I think I'd have to be bending over right in front of you. Check the pic on my website.
JaneT at 1147 today

You have to be registered to comment

Children & Animals

Shelf Life: Shift-It

It would be fair to say that the pet excrement disposal industry is a bit of a sleeping giant. The British are only gradually beginning to take personal responsibility for their dogs' business, but stiff fines and increasing public intolerance will some day make cleaning up after your pets in public a grim civic duty. Any product that promises to ameliorate the essential disgustingness of this chore will surely have a future.

Into this marketing breach comes Vetzyme's Shift-It pet waste "freeze" spray, nothing less than "the first specially formulated product with a unique triple action to aid the fast and effective removal of pet waste". Shift-It freezes turds into easily retrieved nuggets, even while it deodorises and disinfects the scene of the accident. It works indoors and outdoors, protecting pet owners against infection, disease and unpleasantness.

With these bold claims, however, come several caveats. "Not suitable for wet or runny pet waste", reads the small print on the back of the can, and further down there's more disappointment: "Vetzyme Shift-It is NOT designed to 'freeze' pet waste rock solid, but to provide a suitable 'crust' to enable fast, hygienic and effective removal." Vetzyme's product manager, Richard Musgrove, says it is not possible under health and safety guidelines to produce a spray that freezes things solid. "We've produced something that will take the waste from being body temperature to being as cold as possible, as quickly as possible," he says, "so that when you pick it up with a bag or a scoop, you're doing it in one motion, rather than a number of attempts." To assist the process, the instructions also suggest that pet owners "allow faeces to cool for approximately 1 minute prior to spraying". Not a big inconvenience, perhaps, but you wouldn't want anyone coming up to you and asking what you were up to during that one minute. You wouldn't want to have to say, "I'm just waiting for this faeces to cool".

The Shift-It can has a handy chart showing approximate spray times for different pet weights, suggesting a 10-15 second blast to freeze the output of a 10-20kg animal. After some back-garden experimentation, I came up with a much simpler formula: one turd, one can. I used the entire contents trying to freeze up a single example. Even then the promised white crust failed to appear, and after several minutes the faeces in question was only marginally more solid than a nearby control group. In the winter, of course, pet waste freezes all by itself, if you're patient.

On the back of the Shift-It can one finds this note: "Original product concept invented by Kevin Sax". Hard to believe, but there it is. Someone is asserting his moral right to be identified as the author of a dog shit spray.

Shelf Life: Chinchilla Cocktail

Can you believe they're selling this stuff openly, right in the middle of London? Anyone can just stroll in off the street and purchase a box of chinchilla cocktail: a noxious-smelling concoction – made, presumably, from ground-up chinchillas – that claims to promote health and longevity. Along with monkey glands, dried bears' penises and powdered rhino horn, the very existence of chinchilla cocktail is shocking evidence of the limitless cruelty that people will inflict in the name of greed and vanity.

Or at least that's what I thought at first. It just shows you how important it is to read labels carefully before giving vent to any outrage. A closer look revealed that chinchilla cocktail is actually for chinchillas. So once I realised that I was in a pet shop and not some weird voodoo emporium, all the bones and dried pigs' ears lost their evil connotations, and the backroom full of screeching birds didn't seem quite so creepy. A place like this ought to have a sign outside saying PET SHOP in big letters, so that people don't get the wrong idea. Don't worry: I checked, and it does.

So, chinchilla cocktail is nothing more sinister than a wholesome snack with which to spoil one's chinchilla. "Mix one to two teaspoons with staple food daily," say the instructions, "or feed by hand as a special reward." As a special reward for what, exactly? What sort of heroics might one reasonably expect from a chinchilla? Are they capable of alerting their owners to danger, or performing tricks? An investigation into the world of chinchillas reveals that they have two characteristic behaviours: chewing through electrical cable and crapping everywhere. On the face of it there doesn't appear to be much difference between keeping a pet chinchilla and having a rat problem.

Neither does there appear to be much difference between spoiling a chinchilla and keeping it alive. These stocky, big-eared South American mountain rats are very delicate, and perpetually on the verge of crossing to the other side of the veil. Chinchillas need daily exercise, constant temperatures, regular dust baths in specially formulated chinchilla dust and clean bedding made from wood shavings (no fruit trees, no pine). In return for this loving care they will bite you and then die of heat prostration. So why not brighten up their bleak little lives with the odd chinchilla cocktail? This mixture of rosehips, carob, dried berries and alfalfa meal may sound like a particularly joyless vegetarian breakfast, but it will give your little chinchilla a healthy, glossy coat, which makes the pelt worth more in the end.

Pin the Cheque on the Donkey

At the back of the Donkey Sanctuary's main offices, on Spade Farm near Sidmouth in Devon, three or four donkeys are standing at random angles to one another in a patch of sunlight at one corner of the cobbled court. Each of them is wearing its own, specially made, donkey jacket. Apart from the occasional ripple along their withers, and the intermittent fine-tune swivelling of their ears, they are almost perfectly still, frozen in poses of pained deliberation. To the untrained eye, all donkeys look a bit hungover, and yet these donkeys are arguably among the happiest in England. In fact they are probably the best-looked-after donkeys in the world, perhaps in the history of the world.

These are difficult times for charities. When the recent economic downturn began, the level of charitable giving was only just recovering from a sharp decline in the mid-90s. Now charities are facing shrinking returns on their investments, falling revenues from lottery ticket sales and the possibility that the gloomy outlook will further harden hearts. Already the business sector gives less in real terms than it did a decade ago. Charities have been obliged to look at new ways of funding themselves. They are being forced to rethink the whole idea of what a charity is and does.

None of this, however, applies to the Donkey Sanctuary. It remains wholly dedicated to "the provision of care, protection and/or permanent security anywhere in the world for donkeys and mules". Yes, they do mules too. By any financial measure commonly applied to charities, the Donkey Sanctuary is flush. In the last accounting year for which records are available, it took in £13m. In donations, it receives more than Age Concern, Mencap and the Samaritans.

Dawn Svendsen, who handles public relations for the sanctuary, is showing me around the Slade Farm HQ, where the offices and corridors are decorated with every conceivable form of donkey art. "I've been here five years now," says Dawn, "donkey's years!" She came straight out of college to join the charity founded 30 years ago by her grandmother, the kindly-but-steely Dr Elisabeth Svendsen. Dawn's mother also works for the Donkey Sanctuary, and her father, Paul, is its deputy chief executive. We get into the car and Dawn takes me to see more donkeys: the old donkeys, the young donkeys, the donkeys with breathing difficulties. She shows me the rare giant poitou donkeys, one of which, Hilaire, stands at 15.2 hands and sports 16" ears. She even introduces me to Peanuts, the Blue Peter donkey. Dawn was raised with donkeys and now works with them full-time, but as we drive from field to field she still talks non-stop and with great enthusiasm about donkeys, their habits, their diets, their ailments and their gentle natures. "Just tell me when to shut up," she says.

The domesticated wild ass first came to Britain with the Romans, who used them as pack animals. Elisabeth Svendsen acquired her first donkey, a jenny named Naughty Face, in 1969, while running a hotel in Ottery St Mary with her husband. She joined the Donkey Breed Society and became its area representative. Distressed by the appalling condition of donkeys for sale in Exeter market, she made a decision that would change the course of her life. "I just couldn't believe that donkeys could be treated like that," she says, "so I swore I'd never buy another donkey again, and I'd start trying to help donkeys that were in trouble." By 1973 she had rescued 38 donkeys and decided to register as a charity. A few years later she received a legacy from a woman in Hampshire in the form of 204 more donkeys, necessitating the move to the sanctuary's present location. Over the time that Svendsen's donkey sanctuary has earned the right to be called The Donkey Sanctuary it has taken in – at the last official count – 8,722 donkeys. There are about 3,500 donkeys currently living on its 10 donkey farms, spread over 1,000 hectares, plus a further 1,500 in its donkey-fostering scheme, living with families who meet the sanctuary's exacting requirements. Now in her 70s, Svendsen reckons that the charity looks after nearly three-quarters of the UK donkey population.

The Donkey Sanctuary has a reputation as one of those charities that raises money easily and out of all proportion to the relative urgency of its good works. It is sometimes cited as an example of what the Charities Aid Foundation calls "the eccentric nature of British philanthropy". Fundraisers are slightly exasperated by the donating public's skewed priorities, which routinely put animal charities ahead of children's charities in terms of income. "When people make disparaging comments about them, what they're making disparaging comments about is really the British public," says Tom Monk of Ideal Creative, a charity marketing group. "What's quite hard to swallow is the fact that lots of people out there would rather give money and sympathy to donkeys than to, for example, the children of refugees, or other hard-to-support causes."

According to Paul Svendsen, the profile of the sanctuary's average donor is "probably more female, probably not so much below the age of 50". He says most of the donations come from people of modest means, with an average donation of about £8, although this statistic belies the fact that 70 per cent of the Donkey Sanctuary's income comes in the form of bequests.

The Donkey Sanctuary also suffers from a common perception that it has done its job too well. "It's as if donkeys are now being specifically bred to be looked after by the Donkey Sanctuary," says Joe Saxton of the Future Foundation, a think-tank. "It's no longer clear what donkeys are for." Saxton says his mother wanted to foster donkeys at one point, but was refused by the Donkey Sanctuary because her stables didn't have heated flooring. There are still more than 900 donkeys working on UK beaches – all of them monitored by the Donkey Sanctuary – but, for the most part, people keep them as pets or as company for their horse. Occasionally they're pressed into service for Palm Sunday processions, but this only serves to remind us that when Jesus rode into Jerusalem on the back of a donkey, he was almost certainly violating the eight-stone carriage limit recommended by veterinarians, an infraction that today would have cost the Saviour his beach licence.

Even Elisabeth Svendsen is prepared to acknowledge that

the British donkey is about as well cared for as is humanly possible. "I think we've more or less solved the problem for donkeys here," she says, "because those we haven't got, we know about. We've got 60 welfare officers going round the country all the time." But she is still faced with the long-term care of an ageing donkey population at her sanctuary. The average lifespan for a donkey is about 28 years; Donkey Sanctuary residents have an average age of 38; the oldest is 54.

Paul Svendsen is now spearheading the sanctuary's expansion into Europe. "There's massive work to do for donkeys in Europe," he says. In Europe they still beat their donkeys. In fact, they still eat their donkeys. In the village of Villanueva de la Vera in Spain, they still insist on celebrating Shrove Tuesday by getting drunk and maltreating a donkey for three hours. In 1987, this was the fate of the famous Blackie Star, christened by the tabloid that bought him from the villagers and arranged for his safe passage to the Donkey Sanctuary. Now, for the first time in 15 years, the Donkey Sanctuary is preparing to import donkeys from Europe again, including one from Greece that had its ears cut off by marauding louts.

The sanctuary also runs mobile clinics in Africa to treat animals for foot problems and parasitic worms. In Ethiopa alone there are 5 million working donkeys. "When I first started working in Ethiopia the average lifespan of a donkey there was nine years. I think it's about 14 to 15 now," says Elisabeth Svendsen. "It's been brilliant for the economy. It really has made a difference." Similar projects are running in India and Mexico. "Haven't got as far as China yet," says Svendsen. "There are millions of donkeys there."

Back at home Svendsen has also set up the Elisabeth Svendsen Trust (EST), a separate charity that employs sanctuary donkeys to provide riding therapy for children with special needs and disabilities. EST raised £1m last year. "When I started the children's charity everybody said, 'You won't get money. You don't get money for children,'" says Svendsen. "But we do."

A simple, undeniable truth lies behind the Donkey Sanctuary's unstinting success: people like donkeys. Approximately 300,000 people visited the sanctuary last year. During its Donkey Week, held each May, holidaymakers pack out the local hotels in order to spend seven straight days in the company of donkeys. Much is made of the therapeutic power of the donkey at the sanctuary. Dawn showed me extraordinary pictures of bedridden pensioners being visited by donkeys. None of them seem the least alarmed at seeing a donkey by their beds. Perhaps they've learned to keep their mouths shut about such things.

While there may be some justification for criticising the British public's overriding affection for cuddlier causes, the Svendsens' charity can hardly be blamed for its own success. Snobbishness about its aims overlooks the fact that the Donkey Sanctuary is run with exemplary propriety. Reserve funds are in keeping with Charity Commission guidelines (about double annual revenue) and administration costs amount to a modest 5p in the pound. There is no charge to visit the sanctuary – open to the public 365 days a year – and walk its paths dotted with plaques commemorating dearly departed donors. "I think if people are going to leave money, they like to feel they're going to be remembered after," says Svendsen. "I think that's a big thing."

If we were to judge a civilisation on the manner in which it treats its donkeys, we have Dr Elisabeth Svendsen to thank for making Britain the most civilised nation on Earth. Perhaps this is a useless, even perverse yardstick by which to measure our humanity, but it's hard to think like that when you're standing on a sunny Devon hillside looking down toward the sea, surrounded by lovely, lovely donkeys. And Svendsen has every confidence that money will continue to flow into the Donkey Sanctuary's coffers. "It flows as much as I need it," she says. "I haven't turned on all the taps yet."

Welcome to the NewsRoom at permachat.co.uk, the UK's premier online current affairs forum!

>connecting to server...
Current Host: Pashmina
Current Topic: cute things cats do!!!!

capitalistpiglet: there was no legal justification for war and the govt knew it

BUSHWINS: WE HAVE A RIGHT TO DEFEND OURSELVES FROM TERRORISM

LadeezMan has entered the NewsRoom

capitalistpiglet: how is invading Iraq defending ourselves?

Host_Pashmina: the topic is cats doin cute things like lickin the butter. hi ladeezman

LadeezMan: your the host

Host_Pashmina: cool innit

LadeezMan: how did u get that

Host_Pashmina: i won a bet!!!!

Chris2: 20 minutes and counting, Pashmina

LadeezMan: wot bet

Chris2: that she could spell Kyrgyzstan

BUSHWINS: STABILITY IN THE MIDDLE EAST IS VITAL TO OUR SECURITY

LadeezMan: how could she get that right

Host_Pashmina: I geussed!! its funny cos im not usully a very good speller

LadeezMan: can I be host next

Host_Pashmina: I dont even know wot it is

LadeezMan: its that stuff that makes superman ill

BUSHWINS: FREEDOM IS ON THE MARCH

Chris2: Kyrgyzstan is a central Asian republic, formerly part of the Soviet Union

Host_Pashmina: stick to the topic Chris2 or u will be kicked out!!!!!

LadeezMan: this is serial

capitalistpiglet: do you mean surreal?

LadeezMan: damn. Ill never spell good enough to be host

Host_Pashmina: you have to want it bad

Chris2: 18 minutes and counting

capitalistpiglet: I think the govt should release all relevant documents

Host_Pashmina: piglet yr turn for a good cat storey!!!

BUSHWINS: WHY AM I HERE

capitalistpiglet: OK. when my mother's cat had an operation they made it wear one of those big cones around its head

Host_Pashmina: so sweet!

capitalistpiglet: but he got it off by jamming his head in the cat flap & pulling

Host_Pashmina: cats is v clevver sometimes. then wot happend

Chris2: 17 minutes

capitalistpiglet: he chewed all his stitches out

Host_Pashmina: awwwwwwww

>connection to server has been terminated...

Shelf Life: Big Baby Pop

Just for a moment, try looking at the world through the eyes of a dentist. You are someone who bangs on, largely to no avail, about the disastrous effects of refined sugar on dentine. You explain to your patients how the process works, and you tell them how expensive it will be to put things right. Though it is not necessarily in your best financial interests to do so, you constantly warn parents against giving their kids too many sweets, or too many sugary drinks, or putting a child to bed with a bottle of anything other than water. For the most part, everyone you talk to nods sternly in agreement. It's not as if you're making this stuff up, after all.

Then you go down the road to buy a paper and you see this thing on the counter next to the till. It is a small baby's bottle filled with powdered sugar. The nipple of the bottle is made of hard candy. It is clear from the design of the thing that one is meant to unscrew the top, dip the candy nipple into the powdered sugar, and then suck on it. Remember now: you're a dentist. You stare in disbelief. Is this really being sold to kids, you would think, or did they just put it here to piss me off?

The Big Baby Pop is no ordinary sweetie. It takes more than one kind of sugar to make a product like this one, which contains sugar, dextrose (ie sugar) and glucose syrup (ie sugar). Looking at it one might imagine it contains little else, but the manufacturers have also thrown in a bit of lactic acid and citric acid, presumably to kick-start the whole decay process. Perhaps the healthiest ingredients in the Big Baby Pop are the colourings: juicy orange flavour, for example, contains E100 and E120, which sound terribly threatening but are in fact old-fashioned turmeric and cochineal respectively.

So who is this product for? It is, by its own admission, unsuitable for children under three, "because small parts could be swallowed". That's right, this sweet is not recommended for toddlers because there is a danger they might actually try to eat it. I would also add that anyone over the age of 12 should feel profoundly uncomfortable licking powdered sugar off a teat-shaped lolly. I know I did. As for those of you between the ages of three and 12, you might be interested to know that cochineal is made from crushed-up bugs.

Party Rules

The delusion that children's parties have anything to do with the child leaves you early on, when you first see a large group of one-year-olds strapped into seats around a kitchen table in a creepy simulacrum of a grown-up dinner party. Photos will later show that many of the guests are being held upright by disembodied adult hands, their uncomprehending faces glowing in the light of a single birthday candle. The idea that the kids are enjoying the special day is laughable. If they could give voice to their confusion they would probably say: "What am I doing here? This is not my house, and these are not my friends. I don't have any friends."

By the time a child is able to understand the concept of the birthday party, competitiveness between parents is already the driving force. Children have no innate sense of one-upmanship; they invariably want their birthday party to be exactly like the most recent birthday party they attended. Parents, however, do not like slavish imitation; they constantly feel the need to produce something more imaginative, impressive and fashionable than the other parents, to the extent that British families now spend an average of £82 a birthday party, although £500 is more like the norm in certain parts of north London.

As a parent, you will probably end up bearing witness to the entire gamut, from the perfectly sensible to the totally outrageous, and even if you don't want to compete, you have to find yourself a comfortable point on the spectrum. The following is a basic guide.

Presents

The general rule – and yes, rich people, it applies to you – is that a birthday present for a child under the age of 11 should cost no more than £10. This rule is widely flouted, however. The current scene is characterised by an orgy of ungrateful excess, with one expensive gift after another being ripped open at alarming speed by a child who never even pauses to see who it is from. The choice of present, too, is enough to make you nostalgic for crappy plastic. Increasingly, children seem to be requesting, and receiving, grown-up merchandise: DVD players, iPods, professional sporting equipment, makeup, jewellery, etc.

Party bags

It is said the average party bag, traditionally a take-home package containing a few non-robust novelties, some sweets and a slice of cake, now costs an average of £7.48 a bag to assemble. This is even more ridiculous when you consider that the whole point of a party bag is to achieve some kind of economy through bulk-purchasing. You buy a huge sack of sweets and a jumbo bag of useless miniature yo-yos for a couple of quid and distribute the items accordingly: £7.48 is about how much you should be spending all together, bags included.

Slowly, however, toys that were once considered suitable as birthday presents – a Tamagotchi, say – begin to migrate down the gift ladder. Soon the Tamagotchi is only good enough to be the main prize for pass-the-parcel (which now has to be larded with smaller treats, and the game has to be micromanaged so that every child gets one). Then the Tamagotchi is relegated to a mere party-bag favour, one of many. This migration continues until, eventually, your child comes home with a bag containing a remote-control flying saucer and two tickets to see Arsenal play Bolton. If you try to stay off this treadmill, you run the risk of sending your child to a birthday party with a present that may well be inferior to the one they give to the second runner-up in musical chairs.

Fortunately this trend tends to level off after a while, when parents start to see the birthday party circuit for the relentless, wasteful grind that it is. By the time your children hit 12 you should have convinced them that party bags are for babies and spoilt Oscar nominees. If they don't listen, then you simply are not being squashing enough.

Entertainment

Children's parties are about the only time in your life when you would voluntarily allow someone who reminds you of Archie Rice into your home, but in the course of a two-hour party, a 20-minute period where someone else is in charge may well be worth the money. Traditional entertainers are problematic – many young children are frightened of clowns. My son Johnnie, for example, had a fear of people dressed in large-headed character costumes; he once had a panic attack caused by proximity to a life-sized Bob the Builder. Nowadays, DJs, magicians and face-painters are more the norm, but examples of excess and weirdness in this arena are widespread. One London mother reports a sighting of an animal entertainer "with a real meerkat".

Note that entertainers are, generally speaking, wasted on younger children, who would far rather spend the 20 minutes wrecking your house.

Outings

The popularity of birthday outings tends to be governed by cyclical trends. Bowling, ice-skating, swimming, indoor adventure playgrounds, indoor climbing centres, organised football – every venue takes its turn to be of the moment for a particular age group, except, in my experience, the National Gallery. At the grotesque end of the range, parents hire out whole toyshops and let the children indulge in a consumerist free-for-all.

The appeal of the outing is twofold: most tend to include food, which means that for a flat fee you can put the whole hideous experience into someone else's hands, and, second, the enormous expense per head allows you to shave the guest list to a hardcore group of friends in order to make it affordable.

Be aware that when you are dealing with an outing, logistics are as big a consideration as expense, as anyone who has ever tried to take 20 seven-year-olds to a movie by bus will understand.

Food

This is one where excess spending is always in inverse proportion to the guests' happiness. Children want buns, sweets, Hula Hoops, crisps, jelly, Smarties, fizzy drinks and the most vile sort of cocktail sausage available. They don't care about the percentage of cocoa solids in the chocolate and they are not interested in where your bread comes from. You just need enough junk to make everybody feel queasy, and a bowl of carrots for throwing.

There are two directions parental competitiveness can take

here: homelier-than-thou and greener-than-thou. The first lot make a show of Nigella-style domestic perfection, the second make sure that napkins are recycled and the Fairtrade logo is always facing outward.

Themes

This is where you get your own back: by declaring a theme – pirate, fairy, superhero, whatever – you are essentially forcing the other parents to make or buy a costume at short notice, a costume on which you can pass judgment by awarding a prize for the best one. This is not far off charging a fee for attendance, which is where I think we are heading anyway.

Equipment hire

This is to be discouraged generally, although I will admit that we once hired a bouncy castle and, because it was raining, we blew it up in the sitting room, where it touched all four walls and the ceiling when fully inflated. It was a tremendous success and when everyone went home I bounced in it on my own for an hour and a half. If you're going to explore this avenue, shop around for the best price and for God's sake don't tell the man at the hire shop that you want to put it up inside.

Jog With Your Dog

Though I do it religiously three times a day, I would hesitate to call my shuffle around the park with the dog exercise. She gets exercise; I just get cold. Still, if I have to be out there anyway, it makes sense to kill two birds with one stone.

"Petsercise" is a man-and-beast fitness programme designed by the Pet Health Council and spelled out in a 17-page pamphlet called Get Fit with Fido. The programme strikes me as being fairly dogcentric; it says that if we're going to exercise for more than 30 minutes I need to bring a bowl and some water. I have no intention of doing either. Armed with a printout of the pamphlet, we head for a patch of green where we are not known. Cleaning up after the dog at the park entrance requires the untimely sacrifice of pages 1 to 5. I skip ahead to jogging.

Jogging with your dog is a pretty straightforward petsercise – one I could probably have come up with myself – but my dog has never seen me run before, and she is alarmed by it. She dashes back and forth across my path barking, unsure what to do. Then she decides that if I'm running, I must be quarry, and she makes a concerted effort to bring me down. People with normal dogs are staring.

I stop and flip through the pamphlet. It suggests I construct an obstacle course so that we can do "circuit/agility training" together, but I have neglected to bring any PVC tubing to make hurdles. All I brought was a ball on a string and a Frisbee.

The pamphlet says, "Your dog will chase the Frisbee and bring it back to you", but this is not my experience. She chases the Frisbee and runs away with it. I'm supposed to do forward lunges until she returns. I do them until it becomes clear she isn't coming back. So I throw the ball. She chases the ball with the Frisbee in her mouth, then stands guard over both and emits a low, aggressive growl whenever I get too near either. We end up in an unseemly tug-of-war over the ball. Then a labrador runs up and makes off with our Frisbee. I'm getting exercised all right. I decide it's time to go home and pour myself a nice bowl of water.

Ten Ways to Ignore Father's Day

1 Do not lie in. Remember: as far as you're concerned, this is just an ordinary Sunday. By the time your children pile into your bed to shower you with cards and kisses, you should already be downstairs on your second cup of coffee.

2 Ignore any references, direct or oblique, to the "special-ness" of the day. If any member of your family mentions the words "Father's Day" or attempts to confront you about your "odd" behaviour, shout at them for leaving the refrig-erator door open. Don't forget to re-open the refrigerator door afterwards.

3 De-emphasise your importance as a parent by saying things like, "Hey! Here comes Mum! Isn't she great?" or "When I think of the sacrifices that woman has made, I mean, whoa!" Try to sound spontaneous.

4 Refuse to open any cards or presents that are given to you. Your children will probably find this a bit disappointing; some sensitive youngsters may even cry. This isn't your fault. They've been brainwashed. Your wife may start to shout at you, accusing you of insensitivity. She has been brainwashed too. It should be obvious that you are doing the right thing. Your children are crying and your wife is screaming at you. How ordinary does a Sunday get?

5 Make a list of unrewarding chores. On a normal Sunday this would usually be done for you, but you cannot count on your brainwashed spouse sticking to the routine. Think sanding, digging, unblocking drains.

6 Your family may have planned a big Sunday lunch in honour of the "occasion", so excuse yourself, go into another room and worry about things. Bring some tax paperwork with you if it helps.

7 Take your kids to a crowded DIY outlet to purchase some of that metal carpet edging. Allow them to get completely out of control. Wait until all eyes are on you, then put your hands to your head and shout, "Oh my God! I'm hopeless!"

8 Spend the evening thrashing your children at board games in order to teach them hard lessons about the real world.

9 Send them to bed early. In lieu of a bedtime story, tell them about a real incident from your past in which you figure as a terrible moral coward.

10 Forget to ring your own dad. Just like last year.

Shelf Life: Pussy Lawn

Do cats eat grass? Of course they don't. I have seen my own cat eat many things, including mice, dog food, Frosties and endangered songbirds, but I don't believe I have ever seen him eat grass. Which is as it should be, because cats don't eat grass. Cows eat grass, but not cats. It's like one of those easy questions from the opening rounds of Who Wants To Be a Millionaire?. Which of the following do cats not eat? I know what I'd say: I'll take D, Chris. Grass.

Then I find this cat grass in the pet shop, and my whole world turns upside down. The excitingly named Pussy Lawn (every week several would-be porn stars must be disappointed by a trademark search) is in fact a kit for growing your own cat grass, a tray filled with seeds and what appears to be cat litter – "just add water". The packaging claims that cats love grass, which I still find hard to believe. It seems very unlikely they would choose it over a wounded finch. It also says that other animals enjoy it as well, but it doesn't go into specifics.

I raised myself a crop of this so-called cat grass, watering the pre-seeded litter tray and leaving it in a cupboard for a while. Within a week I had a nice green Pussy Lawn, but the cat showed absolutely no interest in it. I shoved it in his face a few times, perhaps a little too aggressively in the end, as he buggered off for the rest of the day and most of the night. I left the Pussy Lawn in the back garden, on the regular lawn, but the cat never goes anywhere near it, and no other animal has given it so much as a nibble.

Trying to track down information about Pussy Lawn over the internet presents an obvious difficulty. Any search engine you might care to use throws up thousands of unsavoury sites, none of which have anything to do with lawns. I did, however, eventually find another proprietary cat product called Kitty Grass, which appears to be the same thing. Cats are apparently mad for it. Reptiles also like it and rabbits find it so addictive that one is advised to limit their intake. It's actually a blend of wheatgrass, barley, oats and rye grass, designed to provide cats with "a tender and tasty source of protein, vitamins, nutrients and chlorophyll" and it's said to help with furballs. So there you are, another lazy preconception shattered. I'd like to change my answer, Chris. I'll go for C, paint.

My Life as a Penguin

They cannot come to you, so you must go to them, trekking ever southward. The cold is unrelenting. Most days the sun barely makes an appearance: at midday the contours of the coast are shrouded in a dismal, leaden twilight, while curtains of icy rain undulate across the bay. When I finally arrive, it feels as though I've reached the edge of the world. This is Torquay, surely one of the most inhospitable places on the planet.

Not if you're a penguin, though. For the black and white inhabitants of Living Coasts, Torquay's harbourside zoo, the term "English Riviera" holds no bleak tinge of irony, even during the so-called "shoulder season", the brief interlude between peak and off season. As far as they're concerned, this is beach weather, and the penguins are out doing what they do best: standing around in a big huddle looking in the same direction, in this particular case at me. I am sitting awkwardly on the sand just downwind from them. Here's something they don't tell you about penguins: they smell. After a brief standoff, the whole group takes a tentative step in my direction. I must be patient.

Barring a last-minute monkey uprising, 2005 looks set to be the year of the penguin. Credit for this goes to a single film, March of the Penguins, an 80-minute French documentary about the breeding habits of emperor penguins in Antarctica, which became an unlikely summer blockbuster in America, and the second-highest-grossing documentary (behind Fahrenheit 9/11) of all time. The film follows the emperors' annual 70-mile trek inland, where they pair up and mate as winter is setting in. The female lays a single egg that the male must balance on top of his feet until it hatches, while enduring 100mph winds and temperatures of -57C. The mother then treks back to the edge of the ice to feed, while the males ... well, I don't want to spoil it for you.

None of the penguins currently staring at me are emperors. Only two places – the Sea Worlds of California and Ohio – keep emperor penguins in captivity. Living Coasts has 71 African, or jackass, penguins, plus 13 gentoos (native to South Georgia Island, the Antarctic peninsula and the Falklands), and a dozen or so newly arrived macaroni penguins. The macaronis, so named after the dashing yellow eyebrow feathers that make them look like Denis Healey in black tie, are isolated for now, but the African and gentoo colonies rub along on the same stretch of pretend beach, sharing the same pool of treated seawater pumped in from the bay. Above us, inca terns wheel about under the nets that cover the site. A few hundred yards into the bay, local cormorants perch on a large, shit-covered rock, keeping it real. The penguins edge closer to me, partly because they are naturally inquisitive, and partly because I'm sitting next to a keeper, Lois Rowell, and she has a big bucket of fish.

When March of the Penguins was released in America it became not just a hit, but the subject of intense political debate.

In the US the religious right is in the habit of rating films in terms of moral content (Kiss Kiss Bang Bang, for example, which features a gay kiss, is rated "abhorrent" by one reviewer). A nice penguin documentary was always going to rate highly with "red state" religious conservatives, if only for what it lacked in terms of profanity, drug references and express promotion of a homosexual worldview.

But the American family-values lobby found something else in the penguins' struggle for survival: role models. The conservative film critic Michael Medved called March of the Penguins "the motion picture of the summer that most passionately affirms traditional norms [such as] monogamy, sacrifice and child-rearing". Other commentators saw it as a parable of Christian faith and forbearance. Church groups block-booked cinemas and held post-screening discussions, much as they did with The Passion of the Christ. One reviewer, writing in the Christian periodical World Magazine, maintained that the film presented a case for intelligent design, the pseudoscience that holds that evolution alone cannot account for certain complexities in nature. This dopey assertion was echoed on various web forums: "It's hard to watch a film like this and not see the evidence of a designer," wrote one viewer.

The backlash that followed proved, if nothing else, how little the American religious right knew about penguins. It was noted (in the film itself, among other places) that emperor penguins are monogamous only for the duration of one breeding cycle;

about 85 per cent will find a new mate next time around. While their childcare is in many ways exemplary, they tend to affect a certain nonchalance when their young are being eaten by petrels. As if this weren't enough, it transpired that Central Park Zoo in New York had a resident pair of gay penguins, Roy and Silo, who were devoted parents to an abandoned egg.

As for the claims for intelligent design, even conservative pundits such as George Will point out that the emperor penguins' reproductive practices seem, if anything, a little ill thought through. Antarctic penguins provide ample evidence of evolutionary development because the DNA record for a single species, preserved in frozen penguin bones, can be traced back thousands of years. The film's director, Luc Jacquet, was quick to distance himself from his anti-evolution fanbase. Commenting on the controversy, Laura Kim, the vice-president of the film's US distributor, said with transparent exasperation, "You know what? They're just birds."

Perhaps so, but the tendency to attribute human qualities to penguins is almost irresistible. "My theory is that it's because they have a recognisable human shape," says Phil Knowling, Paignton Zoo's press officer. "I used to work at an owl sanctuary and we had the same thing with owls."

March of the Penguins is certainly guilty of its own measure of anthropomorphism. The film casts the emperors' struggle as a love story, and Morgan Freeman's sonorous narration often strays into sentimentality. It could have been worse: in the original French version, actors were used to give voice to the penguins. The birds plighted their troth in the language of love.

Zookeepers are not keen on this sort of over-identification with penguins, but that doesn't mean they're immune to it. "You've got to admire them in certain ways," says Tony Durkin, the senior keeper at Living Coasts. "They're characters. I think they have the ability to survive no matter what." But can we learn by their example? Should we be more like the penguin? "We could be more like the penguin, yeah."

In terms of setting an example, the penguins of Living Coasts are a damn sight more faithful than emperors. All three species tend to mate for life, although break-ups are not unknown. "There have been three divorces since I've looked after them," says Rowell, who accompanied the African penguins when they came to Living Coasts from Paignton Zoo and has 20 years' experience with them. There has even been the odd scandal, as when Mr Pops got himself a girlfriend. "He used to visit her when Mrs Pops was incubating," says Rowell, before going on to tell me about the time another penguin left his wife with two babies. Although "that is the exception", she says.

Most of the birds look alike to me, but Rowell has no trouble pointing out Charlie, Vinnie, Ruby, Silent Bob. African penguins have a spray of black dots on their bellies in a pattern unique to each individual. It is impossible, however, to tell males from females without performing an internal examination or a DNA test. "Otherwise we just wait until they mate," one keeper tells me. "The one on the bottom is the female." That's assuming it is a male-female pairing: DNA tests on some infertile penguins at Bremerhaven Zoo in Bremen revealed that several of their supposed breeding pairs were same-sex couples.

The three species at Living Coasts live for up to 20 years in the wild, and longer in captivity. The gentoos and Africans both nest, although the Africans tend to burrow under vegetation, while the gentoos make do with slightly sorry-looking nests made from pebbles. Different species have different sleep habits – some sleep in their burrows, some (such as emperors) standing up, the beak tucked under the flipper. It is supposed that certain types of penguin must actually sleep at sea, although this has never been observed.

By now the penguins have gathered round the bucket and a few have wandered over to size me up. They stare, they circle, they stretch their necks. "The neck-stretch thing is, 'I just don't know what to make of you,'" says Rowell. Occasionally one will tilt back its head and bray like a donkey. One of the small Africans leans in and tugs on my trouser leg with his beak. Two others take turns pecking my right shoe. A fourth penguin ducks under my arm and tries to take my pen. Penguins have an insatiable curiosity that, when you are its subject, borders on harassment. It's like being threatened by a gang of eight-year-olds.

Later on Durkin shows me how to feed the penguins, but it's not as easy as it looks. The fish – mostly sprat and herring – have to go in head first, scales pointing backwards, because the penguins have barbed tongues. Most penguins like the fish to be introduced from one side of the beak or the other, and the operation involves me putting my fingers closer to a penguin's mouth than I am comfortable with. I wonder if they bite, but don't like to ask. It turns out I don't have to, because the penguins bite me.

I persist, however, because I really want the penguins to like me, even though I know they are just birds with the same intelligence as parrots. They don't seem like birds to me, which is good because, as a rule, I don't enjoy being proximate to birds. I don't think I'd be very happy sitting on the ground surrounded by 84 large crows.

I also know that it's a rare privilege to be allowed to sit on the sand with them. Human/penguin contact is normally kept to a minimum. "We try to keep everything as natural as possible here, so we don't build up a general rapport with any of them," says Durkin. "If you wanted to do that, you could, but it would have to be undertaken deliberately, which would be something we don't agree with doing here." I understand perfectly. Can we put hats on them?

Our tendency to identify with penguins may be irrational, but it's probably why we go to see them. "Anthropomorphism is one of those things that works for and against zoos," says Knowling. "Zoos are so important in terms of conservation, and yet we earn our money through visitors." Living Coasts has fur seals, puffins, red-legged kittiwakes and rare bank cormorants, but the penguins are the main attraction. "These guys are ambassadors for their species," says Durkin. "They will show people very closely what they look like. We show how they feed, we explain their life, where they come from, and that builds up a picture for people who can't get down to Antarctica to see them."

The penguins aren't just here to pull in the punters, however. "These birds have quite a gene pool," says Durkin. "If anything ever did happen to the wild population, we could theoretically return birds to the wild again." African penguins are presently endangered, largely owing to overfishing, loss of habitat and oil spills. Macaronis and gentoos are classified as threatened.

Toward the end of my time, one gentoo – Ronnie, I think – sidled up, stood alongside me and started looking in the same direction as I was. Together we stared out over the bay, past the cormorant rock, toward Brixham and Berry Head. After a moment he leaned gently against my shoulder. I resisted the urge to put my arm round him. We stayed like that for a while; me and Ronnie, my special penguin friend. I wonder if they have one his size in the gift shop.

'Downward Dog, Dad?'

I don't have a problem with children doing yoga, but it does strike me as odd. Yoga, in my limited understanding of the discipline, seems designed to fix things that kids, by and large, don't have wrong with them. Websites offering information about yoga for children talk about how it helps them increase their flexibility and cope with stress. One has this testimonial from a newly relaxed child called Daisy: "I feel like a pretty flower floating on the water." My children rarely complain about how stiff they are or how much stress they're under, and if they did I'd say: "Trust me. It gets much worse."

Yoga for kids is nevertheless big business. Triyoga in London has courses for children as young as five. Some of the junior yoga DVDs on offer target three-year-olds. As a babysitter, a friendly TV yoga instructor is probably preferable to the Pokemon movie, but one wonders whether it's a good idea to teach children that this is how exercise is done. Perhaps they should just go out and play.

Still, I can't imagine it doing them any harm, and it seems as if I'm well behind the curve on this topic: when I raise the idea of doing yoga with my seven-year-old son, Will, being careful not to mention that it will make him feel like a pretty flower floating on the water, he says he already does yoga. Really? "Used to," he says, on his way to the fridge. "At school. A person called Mrs Usher came and taught us." What did it consist of, exactly? "Learning these things like cat and dog moves. It was weird." He pauses to give me an impromptu demonstration of Downward Facing Dog, hands and feet on the floor, bum pointing at the ceiling. "Then you start barking like a dog," he says.

What is yoga for? I ask him. "Your body. So your backbone and your hip and your spine can move a lot. And it calms your mind down. And breathing. You won't be able to breathe properly if you don't do yoga."

I still don't believe that he will show any interest in it as an extra-curricular – or indeed, father-and-son – activity. I doubt he will think much of the kids' yoga kit I have ordered from Gaiam Direct: basically a DVD and a gym ball with a picture of Scooby Doo on it and the slogan "Doo Yoga". As a fitness regime, however, it manages to combine two of his favourite pastimes: lying on a big rubber ball and watching TV. I thought I might join in, but by the time I tracked down my own gym ball he felt he had conquered the techniques, and was reluctant to revisit past challenges, preferring to lie on the ball and watch Deal Or No Deal instead.

It was another few days before I persuaded him to show me the ropes. The DVD features a creepily enthusiastic American woman as the guru and six kids on gym balls as our virtual ashram. There is no talk of chakras or prana or of achieving union with the divine by integration of mind, body and spirit; just a few cheery exhortations to sit up nice and straight.

"You start off on an exercise and then you do a game and

then you go on the real yoga," says Will, who has more or less memorised the 30-minute session. We sit on the balls and follow along, stepping to the right, to the left, standing up, picking up the ball and throwing it in the air. I have over-inflated the Scooby Doo ball slightly; Will's feet barely touch the floor when he's sitting on it, and after the fourth time he rolls off across the room I have to pause the DVD to let some air out. It takes a while to get to what Will calls the "real yoga": hands on the floor in press-up position, feet on the ball. We are attempting to roll ourselves back and forth from ankles to knees and back again.

This is an exercise that I have done at the gym many times, although I have always slightly cheated (the trainer can't look everywhere at once), and as a result Will is much better at it than I am. "Just don't drop your hips," he says, echoing the woman on the DVD. Then we lie back with our heads on the ball and our feet on the floor. "This is really hard," he says.

I had worried that my son might be a bit young for indoctrination into the mysteries of this ancient discipline, but halfway through the DVD I'm beginning to wonder if he's actually getting enough yoga with his workout. I want to tell him that there's a whole spiritual element that's not being addressed by this grinning woman.

When I ask him what he thinks of it, however, he shrugs his shoulders and says, "I liked it". I point out that, despite his use of the past tense, there is still about 10 minutes left to go on the DVD. He shrugs again, rolls forward slightly on the ball, pushes eject and deftly exchanges the disc for SpongeBob Squarepants: The Movie. His breathing slows. His lower jaw slackens gently and comes to rest on the ball. As does mine. And relax.

The Chimpanzee Bill of Rights

We, the chimpanzees of Britain, in respect of our impending reclassification as members of the genus *Homo*, according to the US journal Proceedings of the National Academy of Sciences, do hereby assert the following basic freedoms, privileges and legal protections under the law:

- No chimp shall be administered any substance or made to endure any surgical or cosmetic procedure for the purposes of experimentation unless said procedure or substance has first been tested on Pete Burns, formerly of Dead or Alive.
- No law shall be made to infringe our right to bare arses, and no adult of either species shall be made to wear a nappy under any circumstances, excepting where required by a dress code spelled out clearly on the party invitation.
- In accordance with customs governing human life, our inability to read, write, speak or count higher than nine shall in no way prevent us from working at a call centre. And we want an hour for lunch.

- No chimp shall be required to don a bellhop's uniform, wig, fez or straw hat, nor shall he be compelled to ride a tricycle, smoke a pipe or pretend to serve tea to his fellow apes for the purposes of human entertainment, unless his agent thinks it will lead to bigger things.

- With respect to past exploitation of chimps for the purposes of human entertainment, immediate and adequate reparations are to be made. Therefore each member of the species will be furnished with a golf cart with a top speed of not less than 30mph and a stick with a boxing glove on the end. Why is none of your business.

- An end to perceived human superiority in all contexts, be they cultural, legal, scientific, philosophical or spiritual. Del Boy falling through the bar was pretty funny, but you can keep the rest of it.

- No taxation without representation, or failing representation, a banana.

- As full-fledged members of the *Homo* genus, we require the recognition of the fundamental individual dignity and basic equality of not just chimps, but all primates. Except for orang-utans, those fat ginger bastards.

Business & Pleasure

Welcome to the NewsRoom at permachat.co.uk, the UK's premiere online current affairs forum!

>connecting to server...

Current Host: Chris2

Current Topic: Britain's top executives received an average 28 per cent increase in pay last year, six times the national average, even as profits began to slide. Should boardroom salaries be regulated, or even capped, by the government?

Pashmina: did u see that diedre off cornoration street is gettin new glasses

LadeezMan: yup

Bronco: wot abt poshes fake lip ring! Wot a bleedin cop out!!!

Pashmina: exept it aint bleedin

LadeezMan: lol

Bronco: lol

Pashmina: lol @ me own joke!

Host_Chris2: I would like to remind everyone that the NewsRoom is a current affairs chatroom

Pashmina: durh Chris2

Bronco: so wot

Host_Chris2: While you are within its virtual walls, please confine yourselves to discussing *current affairs!*

Pashmina: we are

Bronco: yo Chris2 – how did you make them italics?

Host_Chris2: do you really believe that a pop singer's body-piercings – counterfeit or otherwise – are suitable fare for a serious news forum?

Pashmina: its on the front page

LadeezMan: Bronco, don't you know how to do *italics*

Host_Chris2: yes, but of which publication, Pashmina?

Bronco: how do you it? I want to talk in italics

Pashmina: of all of them!

LadeezMan: italics is EZ *if you know how*

Host_Chris2: if you wish to prattle on about the empty lives of minor celebrities, then may I suggest you visit the StarChamber, or the VIP Lounge, or one of permachat's other dedicated entertainment chatrooms

LadeezMan: those rooms is full of *idiots*

Bronco: TELL ME HOW YOU DO THAT

Host_Chris2: precisely

Pashmina: Chris2 you remind me of somebody

LadeezMan: I know – Chris1

Bronco: maybe he is Chris1. they're never in the same chatroom together

Host_Chris2 : Bronco, you may wish to visit the UserHelp page and click on FAQs. As for the rest of us, I think we should return to the world of current affairs

Bronco has left the NewsRoom

LadeezMan: I see that Michael Barrymore is cruising the Norfolk broads

Pashmina: i thought he was gay

Bronco has entered the NewsRoom

Bronco: cheers Chris2. I found that very *helpful*

LadeezMan: *Nice one M8*

Pashmina: good for you, **Bronco**

LadeezMan: Bold! how u do that pash?

>connection to server has been terminated...

Tropical Islands

From a distance you can't tell what it is, or what it was; this stretched dome, this oblong bubble squatting on the flat, spare landscape of a disused Russian military airbase, deep in the birch and pine forests of the former GDR, just over an hour's drive from Berlin. You can't even guess at its true scale until you get close enough to see the tiny cars parked along its edge.

Here's what it is: a tropical island paradise, with white sandy beaches, waterfalls tumbling into tranquil lagoons, a rainforest, several restaurants, shops and all manner of entertainments, protected from the freezing Brandenburg winter by the world's largest self-supporting hall. Raw numbers aren't much help with something this size, but for the record it's 360 metres long, 210 metres wide and 107 metres high in the middle, enclosing a total interior space of 5 million metres cubed. You could slide the Eiffel Tower in on its side, or, if you prefer, the Statue of Liberty standing up. It's twice as high as the Millennium Dome, and covers a comparable area of ground.

Could this be the future of tourism – sun-kissed leisure without the trouble or expense of travel? Simply recreate the climate and approximate the culture of a popular travel destination at home, then build an enormous car park next to it. We've never had to consider anything quite so utopian – or dystopian – because it's never been practically possible on such a scale. The Centre Parcs bubble is a toy compared to it. If this project is successful there are plans to build more tropical paradises in Europe. Could our own Millennium Dome qualify? Could Bali-on-Thames be a reality?

The idea for this roofed-over resort, called simply Tropical Islands (apparently the German equivalent doesn't sound *sehr gut*), came from Colin Au, a Malaysian entrepreneur. On a visit to Germany, where he happened to be getting four ocean liners built, he noticed that the weather tended toward the foul. He dreamed of bringing the tropics to the Germans, and parking it a convenient distance from Berlin, not far from the main road to Dresden. In Brandenburg did Colin Au his stately pleasure dome decree.

Except, luckily, the dome was already here. It was built in 1997 as a zeppelin hangar by a German company called CargoLifter, which had its own dream of building giant dirigibles capable of floating freight around the globe. This dream went bust in 2002, leaving only debts of €120m (£82m), and a big empty shell. It was one of many grand ventures that have failed to resuscitate the region's moribund economy. Unemployment here is approaching 20 per cent, and recovery has so far proved elusive. A Malaysian consortium fronted by Au bought the building for about £20m, a quarter of what it cost to build. A further £50m has been spent transforming it into a tropical holiday destination, and on the power plant designed to keep the place a balmy 25-28C year round.

On the night of Tropical Islands' gala launch, the transformation from airship hangar to island paradise is nearly complete: there are still a few coiled-up hoses about, and the rainforest plants look a bit dusty, but most things are in place. The sand along the lip of the Balinese lagoon is a pristine white. Round the other side of the rainforest, the island in the centre of the tropical sea – a body of water about the size of four Olympic swimming pools – is set for the premiere of what will be a nightly stage show. The scale of the operation puts one in mind of Willy Wonka's chocolate factory, or a Martian colony, or other things that don't exist in real life. They have trucked in 30,000m cubed of soil and 500 plant species for their rainforest. The speakers that broadcast insect noises are shaped like rocks. And the building itself, it goes without saying, is extraordinary, the biggest inside of anything you will ever see. It makes your head spin. The dome doesn't just have a climate. It has weather. As the place fills up, the extra moisture in the air condenses on the roof. It starts to rain a little bit.

Along the tiered banks of tables running down to the beach, the great and the good of Brandenburg, ambassadors from several south-east Asian nations, regional politicians, local hoteliers and German journalists – perhaps 2,000 people in all – sip at pina coladas and look around with a combination of wonder and apprehension. Everyone wants this place to work, but to many it seems, if anything, slighter madder than the idea of a giant zeppelin factory.

Au steps on to the sand, takes the microphone and launches into a speech, in English punctuated by a running translation, in which he makes a point of distinguishing between the "hardware" of Tropical Islands (beaches, lagoon, rainforest, restaurants) and the "software" (service and hospitality). "People tell me it's hard to get Germans to smile," he says. "Well, we have taught our staff to smile."

After the regional economics minister presents Au with something in a green box, there's a curious interpretative dance-extravaganza-with-boats called Viva Brasil that lasts well over an hour; it's the sort of thing, frankly, you'd expect to endure if Rio hosted the Olympic games. When that's over, the DJ puts on his headphones and the beach party begins. Well-oiled local dignitaries dance in the water with their clothes on. One woman wades in with a lit cigarette. Somebody else breaks a glass in the sand. This paradise is being spoiled by tourism already, and it has even opened yet. How long before they start pulling down the rainforest?

In the corner of the building where the arc of the beach hits the wall, Ingolf Konig is looking on with his son Christof. Ingolf was hired only this morning as a lifeguard – part of the indoor resort's 500 staff – and is positively beaming at his good fortune. He lives two hours away in Saxony, but he's going to look for a place nearby. Christof complains that there is sand in the water slide.

Tropical Islands officially opens for business at 6am the following morning, thence to remain open 24 hours a day, seven days a week, every week of the year. We've heard it is expecting more than 10,000 people on the first day, far more than its maximum capacity of 7,000. By 8am a sign warning of tailbacks from the Tropical Islands exit has already been put up on the motorway, but the motorway is empty. By day the dome perfectly matches the slate-grey sky. There are no queues; visitors are no more than trickling in. A pair of elderly women are drinking coffee under Kenyan-style mud huts on stilts. There are a few dozen people in the water, but the vast majority of the 1,000 or so deckchairs are vacant. The suspiciously tanned Dieter Knabe, a 63-year-old early retiree from Lubbenau, is occupying one of them. "I like it," he says. "For a beginning it's good, but it needs some changes." This is a sentiment one hears over and over again, and one begins to suspect that it's the local equivalent of two thumbs up: OK, needs some changes.

Like what? Dieter indicates the sun projected on the enormous screen behind the sea. "I think it's a little bit simple with the sun and clouds there," he says. "I would like to see some other projections." He makes one other criticism: "It's a little bit fresh." Dieter is a nudist (not permitted here, though wholly unremarkable in eastern Germany) who's just returned from Gran Canaria (hence the tan). He may, by nature, like his beaches warm, but he does have a point: it is a bit parky in here, though that may be partly psychological – outside it's snowing sideways.

He does think the prices are reasonable, however. He's paying €20 (£13) for four hours, plus €1 for every hour over that. By British standards this seems more than reasonable, but East German pensioners such as Dieter are one of the few groups to do well out of reunification; it's their money the leisure sector is after. And even Dieter has brought his lunch in a Tupperware box.

What does he think about Au's all-important "software", the good service and hospitality allegedly as exotic an import to these parts as the rainforest orchids? "They are all very friendly," he says. "It's unusual for Brandenburg because Brandenburgers are stubborn. I think they've had orders."

A few tiers along, another couple have arrived from Magdeburg. They saw the place on the telly the night before and drove 170km to check it out. So what do they think? "The drinks are expensive, but the food is not so expensive," says the wife.

"€2.50 for chicken wings is OK." They, too, agree that it's a little bit fresh. "It could be warmer," says the husband diplomatically.

Further up, a group of steelworkers from Eisenhuttenstadt are drinking beer and larking about after a game of beach volleyball. "It's very interesting," says one. "I know it's the beginning and there have to be some changes, but we are positive about it." Next time they plan to come after work, party all night and sleep in a tent on the beach. You can do that.

They say you will even be able to tan under the dome when the sun is out, though that promise is contingent on the huge fabric roof sections being replaced with transparent material early in the New Year. For now it's a little bit sepulchral under the dome, the atmosphere strangely leaden. The may have taught the staff to smile, but nobody has spoken to the customers; they wander about looking wary and studiously unimpressed. Perhaps they see too much at stake here to feel at ease, or perhaps this really is them at their leisure. The people of the Niederlausitz do not, as a job lot, strike the casual observer as either footloose or fancy-free.

And really, who can blame them? On first sight this place is as bewildering as it is fascinating. The acoustics are weird: laughter and applause don't carry very far in the vast space, but a banging hammer can be heard everywhere. It may seem cheap to most Europeans, but round here, where the population is declining steadily as people leave to look for work, disposable income is hard to come by. And, though I hate to mention it again, the people I talk to keep bringing it up: it's a little bit fresh. One visitor refers to it, only half jokingly, as Tropical Iceland. I spot Au in a corridor talking to a waiter, and take up the matter with him. He says this is a subject on which consensus is rarely reached: some people will always think it should be warmer, some want it cooler. For this reason they make the lagoon warmer than the sea. "We keep the sea cooler for people who want to do laps." But the air, you could make it warmer if you wanted? "Oh yes," he says. "Of course." You can do that too.

Welcome to the NewsRoom at permachat.co.uk, the UK's premiere online current affairs forum!

>*connecting to server...*

Current Host: Chris2

Current Topic: Details of the celebrations planned for the Queen's Golden Jubilee – including an outdoor pop concert and a three-month royal tour – were announced this week, amid worries that a lack of public enthusiasm may scupper the event. Are such celebrations appropriate in this day and age? What do you think?

LadeezMan: I done it once

GordonZola: The jubilee celebrations are money well spent

Pashmina: u had sex with ur teacher!

LadeezMan: I shoud sell my story

Pashmina: how old was u!

nudeguy has entered the NewsRoom

LadeezMan: 29

Host_Chris2: I have to admit I'm very excited abt the Jubilee

Pashmina: 29! wot was she teachin u!

GordonZola: the queen does a magnificant job

LadeezMan: yoga

Pashmina: that does NOT count

GordonZola: she has seen many changes in her 50 year reign

Host_Chris2: Pashmina – you interested in Queen's Golden Jubilee?

Bronco: yoga are u gay

Pashmina: no I never eat puddings

nudeguy: I am nude again right now

LadeezMan: I just said I slept with the teacher didnt I

Host_Chris2: I suppose most of you are too young to remember 1977

Bronco: LadeezMan do u where a leotard

Pashmina: theres lots of men in my pilates class

LadeezMan: no leicester city strip

Bronco: pash r u learnin to fly planes then

Host_Chris2: I was only 8 myself at the time

Pashmina: no PILATES. its like yoga but diffrent

Bronco: is it less gay

LadeezMan: Im not gay! I HAD SEX WITH THE TEACHER

Pashmina: we herd u 1st time

GordonZola: I for one am proud to live in a monarchy

nudeguy: I am also proud. Right now.

Bronco: was ur teacher a man

Host_Chris2: but I can still remember the excitement

LadeezMan: NO

Bronco: r u sure

LadeezMan: I HAD SEX WITH HER

Host_Chris2: & the Golden Jubilee looks set to be even better

Bronco: might of been a ladyboy

Pashmina: leave him be. u cant judge if some1 is gay by there hobbies

Host_Chris2: I've already ordered my commemorative mugs!

>connection to server has been terminated...

Curb Your Enthusiasm

Imagine if there were a sudden craze for building public swimming pools in a country where nobody could swim. A few citizens might pick up the doggy paddle as an urgent alternative to drowning, but the lag between building the facilities and training up the populace would certainly lead to casualties.

Now freeze the water, hand out ice skates to passersby and watch the carnage happen here. I've already seen my first

137

skate-related injury of the year – a friend with a broken wrist who won't be tying his own shoes for the next five to eight weeks – and I have no doubt there will be more. It is accepted that Britain is becoming a risk-averse nation of people with insufficiently dangerous pastimes. So why do they continue to pursue activities for which they have no traditional aptitude with such heedless, headlong enthusiasm?

Did Britons greet the advent of 24-hour drinking with the cautious reluctance of a people who know they're not even very good at 12-hour drinking? Did they heck. Instead of shying away from a challenge, they stayed up all night shrieking and rolling in their own vomit in a game attempt to emulate continental cafe society. Do they stand in the queue for the ice rink thinking: "I've never actually tried this before. I hope I don't shatter my pelvis." No! They're halfway to A&E before second thoughts creep in.

I remember about six years ago visiting a Centre Parcs, the Prisoner-like holiday villages from which cars are banned. It soon became quite clear that most of the adults had not been atop a bicycle for a decade. Everywhere one saw wobbling front wheels, people flying into hedges, pedals crashing into spokes and whole families tipping over, domino-style. This was hardly surprising, given that British officialdom's attitude to cycling could then best be summed up as: "It's not exactly illegal, but as you can see from the way we've laid things out, we'd really prefer that you didn't."

This was also how Britons took to food when, after centuries of British cooking being renowned only for its rigorous approach to boiling, everyone suddenly started trying to make duck liver carpaccio. It's hard to remember that back then we were so bad at cooking that Delia felt moved to write a recipe for toast. No doubt many people were poisoned along the upward slope of the learning curve, but that enthusiasm never abated. Even today when Jamie Oliver makes a seasoning suggestion, the whole nation runs out and buys all the nutmeg in Christendom.

Britons have got better at cycling though, and it's perfectly possible that time and natural selection will turn us into a nation of graceful skaters, but I'm betting that people will be soon looking for more novel ways to hurt themselves. At Somerset House in London they've already erected an ice climbing wall next to the rink for the entertainment of children whose parents haven't seen Touching the Void. My guess is that next Christmas we'll all be naked, fighting with mats tied to our arms like they do in the Royal Marines. I know it looks barbaric and unBritish, but you've got to have a go, haven't you?

PermaBlog – Non-stop comment for a non-stop planet!

Jobseeker's Allowance Should Be For Jobseekers

John Hutton's proposal is about more than shaking a few hard-core layabouts off the unemployment roll; we're talking about a basic principle which must be honoured in tandem with any sort of reform: in a welfare state, those who can work should work, and those who don't must face … *[read more]*

Posted by MaxPersons at 0807 today

Max Persons is the acting deputy director of the Society of Public Policy Institutions Network Research Foundation.

COMMENTS

HEAR HEAR. THERES NOTHING WRONG WITH DEMANDING THAT THE BONE IDLE PULL THEIR WEIGHT
SPECIALRELATIONSHIP at 0911 today

Mathematically speaking this is a pointless waste of time; forcing 100,000 people from the bottom of the ladder into unrewarding (in every sense) employment will save no money and benefit nobody.
SixKindsOfChris at 0915 today

This is yet another anti-blogger initiative. The govt fears our power!

MegaDave at 0923 today

Dear Friends: 2006 has been a wonderful year for the Carroll family, full of joy and surprises. Jan and I celebrated her 60th with a holiday of a lifetime in Mauritius. Cathy's husband Mick is back home with his loved ones while his appeal is being prepared and Joe finally seems to have got his meds sorted out!!! As for me, I finally bought myself a computer, hence this our first fully electronic Xmas round-up. In October young Alex (more like his father every day!) lost the tip of his f

RobertJCarroll at 0938 today

I agree with everything you say Chris. As usual.

JaneT at 1004 today

Forcing us into dead end McJobs is a blatant attempt to silence us. The conspiracy against the armies of truth continues

MegaDave at 1011 today

This has nothing to do with blogging. I maintain three blogs and I still manage to hold down a full time job!

MaxPersons at 1018 today

I'm very sceptical about this plan. Do we really want to scrape the last few no-hopers off the bottom of the barrel and put them into employment? Are computer shop staff not stupid enough as it is?

liberati at 1019 today

That's not very "liberal" of you, "liberati"!

JaneT at 1020 today

We certainly shouldn't be forcing people into work without offering proper support, long-term prospects and a decent wage

SixKindsOfChris at 1025 today

I know. I dare to say what the urban liberal intelligensia only dares think, and I have done ever since I fell off my bike last month.

liberati at 1031 today

THIS ISNT ABOUT HELPING THE NEEDY. ITS ABOUT PUNISHING THE LAZY

SPECIALRELATIONSHIP at 1047 today

I work in a computer shop

MegaDave at 1101 today

---

nger in the salad spinner, but he seems to be managing just fine without it. Finally we bid farewell to our beloved tabby Mr

Bumps in July, when, after a long and happy life, he fell into a peaceful sleep, and Jan backed over him in the drive. Happy Christmas to all! XXX The Carrolls

RobertJCarroll at 1109 today

There's no simple solution, obviously, but neither is the status quo acceptable. What would your advice be, liberati?

MaxPersons at 1122 today

---

always wear a helmet

liberati at 1135 today

You must be registered to post a comment

RIP DIY

Let us not dwell on the mistakes. Let us forget for a moment the shelves that would not support books, or the tiles that fell off, or the doors installed upside down. If DIY is to fade away for ever, then let us remember only the good times. Let us look up, up to the ceiling, to the brown, Australia-shaped stain caused by a leaking upstairs toilet tank, a stain that, thanks to yours truly, has not got any bigger since 2002. I drew a pencil line round it to prove it.

Not all my triumphs are so visible. Who notices the plinth I built to ensure that the new fridge would fit snugly into the old slot? Not many, although I have been known to point it out during dinner parties. As I go through the house, however, I can revisit all my old triumphs. Tiles in the children's bathroom – more than 90 per cent still intact. Nice loo roll-holder placement by the way. Come downstairs. See the way the phone extension cord hugs the skirting board? Not as easy as it looks. Check out the carpet edging in the door frame there. Straight or what?

Although I am by no means good at DIY, and it never fails to put me in a bad temper, I remain devoted to it. In fact, the worse you are at home improvement, the more satisfying it is when it goes inexplicably right. At its best, DIY is a voyage of self-discovery. The bold DIYer proceeds with the idea that all there is to know about roofing felt is contained in the instructions on the back of the label, and that everything else comes from within. That is the difference between DIY skills and actual expertise. For a professional installer, the laying of a rubber floor is not a primeval struggle of man versus glue; it is just a day at work. Perhaps that is why, once I have got good at something, it loses its appeal. That is why one of the cupboard doors under the stairs is fixed, and the other one still comes off in your hand.

Before the advent of the DIY superstore, builders' merchants were too forbidding for the hopeless amateur. In the bad old days, I used to send my wife to buy parts and hire tools, because her wilful ignorance made her impossible to patronise. When the man behind the counter asked what she wanted a wet saw for, she told him it was none of his business.

Then came the superstore. Suddenly a man could stand and stare at hinges for hours without anyone asking intimidating questions about whether you wanted butt hinges or projection hinges. You could just fill your trolley with a whole variety of hinges, the better to meet all present and future hinge needs. The success of such places seemed assured, for even the smallest projects required several return trips. Stalking the aisles of B&Q or Homebase, the DIY-addict discovered strange new solutions to basic problems – miracle sealants, meta-adhesives, novel forms of anchorage, flooring "solutions" – which appeared to allow the unskilled to purchase competence.

Ninety-nine per cent of all DIY work lies within the realm of "making good": plugging gaps, filling holes, levelling cracks – it doesn't have to be pretty, as long as it gives you something to paint over or nail into. My personal collection of making-good stuff is extensive and varied. I have mastics, putties, plasters, resins, mortars, sealants, fillers and hardeners for every occasion. If I see a new sort in the shops, I buy it. Sometimes I mix them.

Despite its perverse pleasures, it is hardly surprising that DIY is on the wane. In a world that is flooded with disposable goods and competent eastern European tradesmen, mending things yourself has become a subversive act, a defiant statement that says you are still willing to pay over the odds for a second-rate job. It is also a fairly thankless pastime. When asked about my DIY skills, my wife will talk not of my former triumphs, but will insist on reminding people of my mishap with the self-levelling floor compound.

But then my wife does not do DIY. She has never got an electric shock while standing on a ladder. She has never slipped and driven the head of a screwdriver into the soft flesh between thumb and forefinger. And she has never known the profound satisfaction that comes from patching in a big hole in the bedroom wall (all the more satisfying if you made the hole yourself in the first place by opening the door too far) with wood glue and wallpaper paste over a latticework of old ice-lolly sticks. I could show you the very spot, but under two coats of paint, you can't even see the difference. Just don't touch it.

PermaBlog – Non-stop comment for a non-stop planet!

We Must Act To Restore Faith in Phone-ins
ITV is right to suspend all programming that uses premium-rate phone lines until a thorough audit has been completed. Viewers need to be reassured that all TV contests and votes are conducted honestly and openly if this growing lucrative industry is to survive … *[read more]*

    Posted by MalcolmG at 0926 today

Malcolm Glennister is the producer of Just Keep Ringing! a pre-recorded phone-in quiz show on ITV Hoopla

COMMENTS

I'm glad all that Iraq business has been sorted out so we can concentrate on the issues that really matter

SixKindsOfChris at 0954 today

I'm sorry if you don't think it's important, but this is an issue of major concern for many people who regularly call premium-rate lines, as well as the broadcasters who use them.

MalcolmG at 1028 today

Premium-rate phone lines are a moron tax, and an issue which is only of interest to morons

liberati at 1046 today

That's a terribly patronising attitude, and one I don't share. How do you define "moron"?

MalcomG at 1050 today

How can you possibly regulate an industry that is itself a scam?

JaneT at 1057 today

Moron – n. a person who calls a premium rate number to vote on which pudding Eamonn Holmes should eat
liberati at 1113 today

I understand that many people's faith in premium rate services has been shaken, but I think it's unfair to deride an entire industry
MalcolmG at 1122 today

I would vote to see Eamonn Holmes eat a bowl of dirt. Does that make me a moron?
ElSmell at 1127 today

Not at all, ElSmell. It makes you a consumer, one whose trust the broadcasters must learn to cherish
MalcolmG at 1131 today

All premium-rate lines are rip-offs. Full stop.
JaneT at 1135 today

Not this one! Try 0900 222 6767 for a guaranteed cash prize every time
bigdaddy090 at 1137 today

No one forces you to ring them, and the revenue they generate

pays for a lot of programming. Without them many shows would not survive.

MalcolmG at 1139 today

What programming? Phone-in shows are the programming

SixKindsOfChris at 1202 today

You mean Ant and Dec could become extinct?

liberati at 1204 today

---

bigdaddy090, that phone number just plays a recording of Jerry Rafferty singing Baker Street. Where's the cash prize "every time"?

JaneT at 1217 today

In my bank account! Ker-ching!

bigdaddy090 at 1219 today

It's people like bigdaddy090 who give our industry a bad name

MalcolmG at 1225 today

Your industry has a bad name because your industry is a bad thing

SixKindsofChris at 1233 today

I would also vote to see him smeared in lard and catapulted into an electric fence

ElSmell at 1242 today

You've got a lot of interesting programming ideas, El Smell. Drop me an email sometime.

MalcolmG at 1249 today

Got a complaint? Call my helpline! 0900 222 3838

bigdaddy090 at 1251 today

You must be registered to post a comment

Food & Fashion

Shelf Life: Nutty Oatios

The naming of breakfast cereals must be a difficult business. Most of the really good names – Corn Flakes, Shredded Wheat, Force – were snapped up before the first world war and by the '70s virtually every permutation using the words crispy, crunchy and sugar had been explored.

These days, new names struggle to capture the shopper's attention while simultaneously sending just the right message about the cereal's putative benefits. One senses the late nights, the snapped pencils and the exhaustive market research behind cautious appellations such as Healthwise, Precise and Weetabix Advantage.

It is refreshing, therefore, to see a product name as devil-may-care as Nutty Oatios. The manufacturer, Mornflake, has gone back to basics with its new cereal, which literally consists of nutty, oaty Os, or "deliciously crispy oat rings with hazelnuts", to give them their full subtitle.

It is obvious that nobody stayed up late coining Nutty Oatios, or testing its impact in comparison to Oaty Nuttios. Clearly there has been no undue worry about "nutty" being a colloquial term for "mentally unbalanced", or pointless focus group hand-wringing over the homophone "otiose", meaning idle or indolent. What's in a name? If they taste good, who cares whether they are called Crazy Lazy-Os or Workshy Lunatix?

The Nutty Oatios box bears a stern preprandial warning:

"Please note: this is a crunchy product. If you are in any doubt about the condition of your teeth, please consult a dental practitioner." Nutty Oatios is in fact a very crunchy, even gritty, product. Ensure your jaw is properly aligned before eating it. It's also a very heavy product, although it is by no means the densest cereal on the market. The same size packet of Alpen actually weighs 50 per cent more.

On close inspection one discovers that each individual oat ring has been forcibly encrusted with nuts and seeds to the extent that in most cases the hole in the middle is clogged up. Occasionally you come across two or more Os bound together into a large nugget of oaten ore. To be honest, Nutty Oatios are all right once you get used to them, a healthy compromise between breakfast cereal and bird food. A banner across the front of the box declares that Nutty Oatios are "also delicious hot", but this seems an unlikely; a bit like claiming that Corn Flakes are also great stale.

According to the box's side panel, Mornflake Oats Limited, of Crewe, has been milling oats in Britain since 1675; up until now, it would seem, in secret. With Nutty Oatios – along with its sister cereal, Triple Chocolate Crisp – the company is clearly making a bid to raise its profile among less oat-conscious consumers. And good luck to it.

Welcome to the NewsRoom at permachat.co.uk, the UK's premiere online current affairs forum!

>connecting to server...

Current Host: Chris2

Current Topic: The Parliamentary Commissioner for Standards, Elizabeth Filkin, has declined to seek reappointment after accusing the government of undermining her office and encouraging a whispering campaign against her. The Tories have called for a full enquiry into the matter. Is the self-regulation of parliament now an impossibility? What do you think?

Pashmina: how can she be a word

LadeezMan: she just is

capitalistpiglet: she's a verb

Pashmina: as in how

LadeezMan: as in I'm just going to Delia this egg

Bronco has entered the NewsRoom

Pashmina: wot does that mean!!!

Bronco: morning rom

LadeezMan: boil it

Pashmina: WHY DONT U JUST SAY BOIL THEN ITS SHORTER

Bronco: room even

LadeezMan: hiya bronc M8. werve u bin

Bronco: just finished a double shitf

capitalistpiglet: actually it can also be a noun

Bronco: shift even

Host_Chris2 has entered the NewsRoom

Pashmina: omilord. as in wot

Host_Chris2: sorry about that. Logged myself off accidentally. Where were we?

capitalistpiglet: as in "she's done a Delia"

Bronco: who r we tlaking abt

Host_Chris2: we were talking about parliamentary standards...

Pashmina: wot does that mean then

LadeezMan: its like cooking in a bitch way

Pashmina: thats stupid

Host_Chris2: OK people, let's return to the topic please

Pashmina: its like having Pashmina in the dictionery

capitalistpiglet: pashmina is in the dictionary

Pashmina: oh yeah under wot

LadeezMan: under p

Host_Chris2: Pashmina, I'm sure you have an opinion on Elizabeth Filkin

Bronco: itsa sort of scraf init

Pashmina: she shoud keep her baby & 4get abt Steve Ping

LadeezMan: thats Liz Herley you Delia

Bronco: scarf even

Pashmina: well who is Liz Filkin then

capitalistpiglet: Bronco is there something wrong with ur keyboard

Host_Chris2: she's the Parliamentary Commissioner for Standards

Bronco: no im just relly durnk

Pashmina: oh that one. I reckon shes done some kind of Delia

Host_Chris2: Interesting. What do you mean by that, Pashmina?

Pashmina: I dont know

capitalistpiglet: she's the first TV personality to enter the language

Bronco: Im about to Rolf

>connection to server has been terminated...

Shelf Life: Sparkling Belly Button

I don't like to buy too many fashion accessories from the corner shop at the end of the road. Frankly, I don't even like to buy butter from there. Let's just say I've had some bad experiences on both counts.

At £1.99, however, the Sparkling Belly Button seemed like a fashion risk I could afford to take. The tiny batteries are included, and when properly fitted the Sparkling Belly Button lights up and flashes red and green, as if your torso houses some kind of hard drive. Normally I would have suspected its actual trendworthiness; by the time they reach the shelves of this humble shop most fashion trends, like most of the dairy products, are well past their sell-by date. I had reason to believe, however, that I might be in the vanguard with the Sparkling Belly Button thing: it was hidden away on the toy rack, next to the plastic guns and the play money. No wonder the folks at Vogue had missed it.

I'm not much of an ambassador for today's midriff-baring styles, nor am I very big on body art. Body art was once more or less synonymous with self-harm, which always put me off a bit, but these days there are plenty of alternatives for the faint-hearted. Fake tattoos are now very sophisticated, and no longer limited to images of Spider-Man. Glue-on nose studs allow self-expression without risk of infection. The Sparkling Belly Button is "non-piercing", applied with double-sided tape. I figured I could wear it under my clothes at first, until I got used to being so trendy.

Unfortunately my Sparkling Belly Button didn't come with any double-sided tape (an oversight) and I was forced to make my own, highly unsatisfactory arrangements. I sprayed the back of it with photo-mount, a product that "may" irritate the skin, which in fact "does" irritate the skin, especially in the delicate umbilical region. Of course the thing doesn't have to go in your navel. "The versatile 'button' can be worn anywhere," said a website I consulted, "the possibilities are endless!"

I'm afraid I suffered what can only be described as a failure of imagination at this point. The possibilites didn't strike me as endless at all. I put it on my forehead, but I had to accept that it was doing me no favours there. For a while I wore it on the palm of my hand, Logan's Run-style, but I think I'm too old to carry off the Logan's Run look: by the rules of that future dystopia, I would have been put down eight years ago.

Even if it doesn't suit me, I must admit the Sparkling Belly Button represents a technical advance in accessorising to rival cut-to-size hologram eyelid tape and mood nail polish. Where science leads, let fashion follow.

Straight Eye for the Queer Guy

The hit American programme Queer Eye for the Straight Guy, in which a team of homosexual men forcibly restyle a drab heterosexual slob, is really a small-scale version of a larger trend: the long-term campification of straight men. But could this transformation work the other way round? Could you find a gay man with a confident sense of style and just take it away? And if it did work, would it be cruel?

Our victim for the day is Andy Butcher, a 25-year-old from Hoxton in London with his own fashion PR company, Laundry Communication. We meet for the first time outside Burtons in Oxford Street. His "look" consists of jeans and an ordinary, if rather snug, hooded sweatshirt worn under a stripy blazer and accessorised with a multicoloured scarf and a woollen visor. It's an inventive yet understated little ensemble: eclectic, simple, effortlessly stylish and wrong, wrong, wrong. Where is the stonewash? Where is the fleece?

Andy says he doesn't really go in for bright colours, which is good. Today we'll be investigating a muted palette: the greys, the blue-greys, the grey-greens, the light blacks. As the "straight stylist" I've done my best to lead by example: I am casually dressed in jeans from Gap and a grey flannel shirt from, well, the laundry hamper. Andy is clearly not impressed, but he isn't here to be. He's here to be transformed.

An initial glance around Burtons proves disappointing. There is stuff here that would have been derided as hopelessly girly just a few years ago. The goalposts for heterosexual fashion shift constantly; even at the macho fringes lie leather goods and accessories that are, looked at another way, dangerously camp. No wonder all the football hooligans have been forced into Burberry. Eventually, however, we begin to find what we're looking for. I ask Andy if he wears much corduroy. "No," he says tersely, making a face at the pre-distressed tan trousers I'm holding up. But these babies go with anything! And they're on sale!

There follows a brief discussion as to whether a long-sleeve T-shirt bearing the legend "Flirt Alert" falls into the "so bad it's good" category, but we decide it doesn't and is therefore perfect. In fact, styling Andy as a heterosexual is really a simple matter of tuning in to a reverse gaydar: if he hates it, we're usually on the right track. "Square-toed loafers," he says with a shudder. "That's a real no-go." A no-go in what size, sir?

Andy's first ensemble consists of the aforementioned cords, the no-go shoes and the Flirt Alert shirt under an anonymous black windcheater, topped off by a New York Yankees baseball cap: nothing says heterosexual like genuine official merchandise. He emerges from the changing rooms looking like someone else. He appears confused, shifty, hunched. By George, I think he's got it! As he stares forlornly into a mirror, it seems as if he might at any moment launch into an anecdote about his air filter catching fire on the M6. Helpfully, I ask him about his car. "I drive a Vespa," he says. We have more work to do.

His second look consists of the cords combined with a heterosexual-style "party shirt". Normally, Andy would dress in clothes that allow him to go straight from work to the watering holes of Hoxton, or to nightclubs such as Radio Egypt, Zigfrid or the Horsemeat Disco. "If I'm going out I think what I'm gonna put on in the morning," he says. "Or go out and buy something on the way." No, no, no: straight men go home and change. Party shirts come in a variety of styles – polka dot, Hawaiian, bowling uniform – but you should only ever own one, so that when you put it on people know you are Ready to Party. Andy's party shirt is an electric blue, oversized houndstooth check affair. He looks very straight in it. I wonder, does he feel a little bit straight? "Actually, I feel a little bit queasy," he says. You will do, at first.

Next we have an American football shirt, number 69. Nice. I instruct Andy to tug the sleeves up to his elbows, and to accessorise with a bland cap. "You look like Chris Martin from Coldplay," says someone. "He's straight," I say. Andy's cutting up rough about the light blue fleece that compliments this outfit perfectly. He thinks XL is too big for him, but there is no such thing as too big, only too small. In any case, a real straight guy would probably have a large collection of free fleeces with insurance company logos on them, and when they're giving them away you can't be too fussy about size. When he puts it on I think he can see that I'm right. It's absolutely shapeless; you could wear anything under it, even pyjamas. And it's warm.

The marvellous thing about the pieces I've chosen for Andy is that they will work together so well, especially after they've been washed together a few times. It's a basic heterosexual capsule wardrobe: devil-may-care without being adventurous, relaxed, safe, down-to-earth and straight as a dye. I don't know why I should feel the need to apologise for it, but I do. Sorry, Andy.

Shelf Life: Inner-Balance Bio Cheddar

It's been a long time since I've run across a coinage as exquisitely stupid as "bio cheddar". The pairing of the word cheddar with any scientific, vaguely futuristic prefix or suffix has a definite comic reliability – hyper-cheddar, megacheddar, cheddartronic, geo-cheddaral, macrocheddar, the CheddarSphere, autocheddar, cheddarogenic – but, um, the result would surely preclude the idea of anyone taking you seriously.

Obviously the people at Anchor do not see it this way. Inner-Balance Bio Cheddar is the latest "functional food" to hit the dairy aisle, functional food being the least disagreeable of a clutch of unsatisfactory terms – foodaceuticals, nutraceuticals, pharmafoodicals – for foodstuffs that have been modified to make them more health-giving. Of course food itself has been shown to prevent death in those who take it regularly, but demonstrating anti-starvation properties is no longer enough. You've got to have an angle.

Inner-Balance Bio Cheddar has been made with additional DR-20TM Lactobacillus cultures, which is to say bacterial cultures of the sort commonly found in cheese, but DR-20TM is a patented, trademarked lactobacillus (Lactobacillus rhamnosus HN001, since you ask) with its own little logo featuring two whirly arrows, the type of thing you'd expect to find on a box of washing powder or the lower left-hand corner of your computer monitor. It strikes me that patenting a lactobacillus is a lot like patenting gin rummy, except that patenting gin rummy wouldn't be allowed. Right now your gut is teeming with bacteria owned by the New Zealand Dairy Board.

Lactobacillus rhamnosus HN001 is a probiotic, or "good", bacterium, which is meant to push out more harmful bacteria and make your intestines a more stable, close-knit community. All this depends on whether the lactobacillus in question reaches your intestines alive, whether it stays alive once it gets there and whether it's frisky enough to indulge in "the competitive exclusion of pathogens". The answers to some of these questions may be found in scientific papers such as "Analysis of the faecal microflora of human subjects consuming a probiotic product containing Lactobacillus rhamnosus DR20", which, for obvious reasons, I didn't read.

As far as real benefits go, the Anchor people only say that "Inner-BalanceTM is a mature cheddar made with increased levels of DR-20TM Lactobacillus, which as part of a healthy diet can help to keep your digestive system in balance", which is a lot like saying that Inner-BalanceTM and 50 cents will get you a cup of coffee. If you happen to suffer from cheddar-deficit disorder, however, this stuff will fix you right up. Recent work at the Institute of Cheddarnautics has proved that. Oh, stop me.

SUSPICIOUS PACKAGES AND EXTENDABLE ARMS

Carole's Corner:
Sort yourself out with help from the Mail on Sunday's new lifestyle columnist Carole Caplin

Dear Carole, I am having a dinner party next week. All my friends are vegetarians, as am I most of the time, but I'm living on light at the moment as part of my detox. Should I put out food for my eating guests, or should they respect my breatharian beliefs while they're in my house? I had another question, but I am too tired to write it down.

Freda, Leamington Spa

Dear Freda, In answer to your second question, I would go with the cape, or maybe something with rainbows on it. As for the first, I always find a bowl of bananas makes a nice compromise in these situations, as long as you're strict with yourself.

Dear Carole, Hi! I know you must get asked this all the time, but what's Cherie Blair really like?

Dave Z, Oxford

Dear Dave, You're right, I do hear that question a lot, from both sides of the spirit veil. All I can say is that Cherie is a very warm and intelligent person, but she has a lot of toxins in her system right now, if you know what I mean. And she knows sweet FA about footwear. I would love to tell you more, but MI6 have planted some kind of chip in my head.

Dear Carole, Last week I had a bit of a freakout while I was channelling with my magnet hat on. My reflexologist says it's because of my wheat addiction, but my Navajo spirit worker says my ancestors are punishing me. Who is right? The stress of not knowing is making my high blood pressure worse.

Runs Like Fire, Hemel Hempstead

RLF, The gullibility of some people astounds me. How many times do I have to say it? There is no such thing as high blood pressure! It's all in the mind. I think the wheat addiction is definitely the source of your problem. Studies have proved that wheat is as addictive as crack cocaine. Try throwing away all your possessions.

Dear Carole, Which shoes go with the celeriac jumpsuit? I've muddled up all the tags!

Cherie, London

Cherie, Don't panic. You can either wear the purple Manolos or those sandals made of nettles. It's all spelled out clearly on my invoice. Focus.

Dear Carole, Last month I met this really great guy. He is attentive and sweet, and there is nothing in the world he wouldn't do for me, but recently I have begun to notice a few little things. For example: he has a weird habit of using a brand new credit card every time he pays for something. Also, he says he was born in Monaco, but has a temporary Haitian passport and the picture in it is a publicity still of Orson Welles dressed as Cardinal Wolsey. Now he wants to borrow £70,000 from me. Am I being paranoid?

Worried in Wolverhampton

Dear Worried, He sounds divine! If you don't want him I'll have him!

Welcome to the NewsRoom at permachat.co.uk, the UK's premier online current affairs forum!

>connecting to server...

Current Host: Chris2

Current Topic: In the wake of the release without charge of 4 British citizens previously held in Guantanamo Bay, the home secretary has proposed new "control orders" restricting the freedoms of terrorist suspects. Are such measures necessary, or are they a dangerous threat to liberty? What do you think?

ilovesuet: its so great

jenni@boughtledger: well it does make for an excellent pie crust

ilovesuet: what does

LadeezMan has entered the NewsRoom

Pashmina: hi ladeezman

LadeezMan: Hi. Wot a coinsidance

Bronco: wot is

jenni@boughtledger: essential for steak & kidney pudding

LadeezMan: I was released without charge yesterday

Pashmina: the drugs thing

LadeezMan: yup

Host_Chris2: let's stick with the topic

ilovesuet: I don't really eat meat

Bronco: coudnt they find no evidence

jenni@boughtledger: thats weird

LadeezMan: they got sick of waitin for me to poo it out

Bronco: nice 1

ilovesuet: what is

Host_Chris2: Pashmina, do you think the new controls are a necessary precaution or a threat to liberty?

Pashmina: both

jenni@boughtledger: that you dont eat meat

Host_Chris2: would you like to elaborate?

Pashmina: no

ilovesuet: whys that wierd

jenni@boughtledger: because your so crazy abt beef fat!!

Bronco: so how long does it take to come out of you

ilovesuet: what!!!!!!!

LadeezMan: dunno. still waitin on a sim card and a £1 coin from before new year

jenni@boughtledger: because you do eat suet!

ilovesuet: youre mad! i'm vegetarian!

Pashmina: me too

Host_Chris2: they're your civil rights people

Bronco: maybe u shoud go to a doctor ladeezman

LadeezMan: thats what the police said

Pashmina: but I do eat chease

jenni@boughtledger: then why do you call yourself ilovesuet?!!!

Pashmina: & chicken

ilovesuet: It's I love Sue T – my fiancee Sue Theophilides

LadeezMan: I can get u a sim card if u want, any phone

jenni@boughtledger: u said u were single

Bronco: thats ok

>connection to server has been terminated...

Camp Coffee

Major-General Sir Hector McDonald (born 1853), the son of a crofter, enlisted with the Gordon Highlanders and worked his way up through the ranks, serving with distinction in the Afghan war and in India. He became known as "Fighting Mac" for his exploits at the Battle of Omdurman, was wounded in the second Boer war and later given command of the troops in Ceylon, where charges of homosexuality were brought against him. He shot himself in a Paris hotel in 1903, after reading about his impending court martial in the New York Times.

He's also the guy on the Camp coffee bottle, the one sitting on a cushion outside a tent, with a Sikh servant standing by with a tray. Actually, they got rid of the tray decades ago, either because it seemed too servile or because it had a bottle of Camp coffee on it, which presented a troublesome conundrum: how could the scene on the label possibly be depicted on the bottle in the scene? And what about the bottle on the label on the bottle in the scene? These are the sorts of questions that occupy the very stoned. No doubt there were letters of complaint from freaked-out consumers.

In any case, the Sikh guy was left standing there as if he didn't know what to do with his free hand, which was clenched into an anxious little fist. Recently, allegedly in response to complaints from Asian shopkeepers, the label was amended further, so that the Sikh and the general now sit side by side, with a cup of coffee each. This change has been described by the Tory MSP David Davidson as "political correctness gone mad".

Everyone is entitled to an opinion, of course, but it's also apparent that Davidson needs to get out more. This is not even an example of political correctness gone slightly giddy. Perhaps if the servant were sitting in the general's lap (and I think this is where we're heading, albeit with excruciating slowness) it might be described as "historical accuracy gone frank", but the story so far – Sikh brings disgusting coffee-and-chicory-flavoured beverage, stands around for 60 years, puts down tray, stands around for another 30 years before deciding to take a load off – is hardly characteristic of the ruthless revisionism normally employed by the PC brigade in order to torture Daily Mail readers. We're talking about a few minor changes, introduced with exceeding caution over a very long period, to the label of a Victorian product that has improbably survived into the 21st century. Complaints about the label's "racism" go back at least six years. The sitting Sikh has been on the shelves for months without anyone taking much notice.

All labels change to suit the perceived tastes of customers; even the ones that seem to have stayed the same for generations have been subtly adjusted. Old-fashioned packaging makes consumers think of botulism, not of Empire. The original Camp label may be preferable to the sort of people who despise all forms of improvement – only they could still be drinking Camp coffee —but as far as I'm concerned the changes aren't happening fast enough. At this rate I may not live to see the Sikh and McDonald's first kiss.

Eating Healthy for Children: New Strategies

Kellogg has been sharply criticised over the marketing of its new Coco Pops Straws: high-fat, high-sugar, chocolate-lined edible straws through which kids are meant to suck milk. Kellogg, in turn, claimed the product "encourages children to eat breakfast". In fact Coco Pops Straws are at the forefront of the incentive-added children's food market. Here are just a few of the brands set to launch this year ...

- **Poker Chips** A great-tasting, extra-salty way for kids to learn the maths behind Britain's fastest-growing indoor sport. Each 500g bag contains an assortment of £1-, £2-, £5-, £10- and £20-denomination oven chips, plus a free deck of cards, strategy leaflet and a helpline number (calls cost 50p a minute, so make sure your parents don't find out).
- **Grand Theft Auto: The Cereal** To what lengths would you go to get your kids to eat a healthy, balanced breakfast? This tasty cereal is made from wholegrain rice and sweetened with natural fructose. It's high in vitamins, minerals and dietary fibre, low in fat, free of additives and carbon-neutral. But the packaging encourages, even exhorts, children to steal cars and shoot cops. So there's a trade-off there. We believe in parental choice. And when we called them Zero Emissions Crunchy Cars they just didn't sell.
- **Jaffa Cake Orange-flavoured Oranges** Acclimatise your children to the look and feel of real fruit with these full-size, cake-filled oranges with tangy sweet peel icing. Just like the real thing, but with three times the vitamin C!
- **Fat-Acceptance Clusters** Full-calorie breakfast nuggets

shaped like little plus-sized people help teach youngsters that the world contains a wide range of different body types, not just attractively thin.

- **Sweet Baby Cheeses** Bite-sized, sugar-frosted nuggets of brie will introduce your children to the joys of a healthy Mediterranean diet, and an aggressively religious marketing strategy ("Do You Believe in Sweet Baby Cheeses?") will see the snack made available free in most C of E schools from September 2007. In strawberry, chocolate and original French vanilla.

- **Cappuccin-Os** The sooner kids learn to love the taste of coffee, the sooner they'll be able to function in the morning without food. Available in regular, wheat-free and lactose-intolerant.

- **Teddy Beer** This sweetened, lightly sparkling alcopop, a tempting combination of dark rum and lager with just a hint of lime, comes in a genuine 12oz baby's bottle complete with sterile teat and collectible Crazy Teddy cap. Despite the controversial packaging, however, a spokesman for the distributors of Teddy Beer denies that the product is aimed at young children, insisting that it has been specifically designed to appeal to pregnant women and the mentally ill.

Geordie Drever Comes to London

The premise of Channel 5's reality TV series, The Farm, is basic: take a clutch of Z-list celebrities (Z being, in the case of Jeff Brazier, a rather generous rating; lucky for him we've run out of alphabet), persuade them to exchange their natural restaurant/nightclub habitat for life on a real, if highly art-directed farm, and see what happens. But what if this premise was reversed? What happens when you introduce a real farmer to the lifestyle of the low-wattage celeb? And will he ever return to the farm after having tasted the life of Rebecca Loos, Stan Collymore and Debbie McGee?

Sadly, none of them are actually at the Ivy the night that the 48-year-old Westray cattle farmer George Drever (Geordie to his friends) makes his debut, dressed neatly in a black Westray rugby club shirt, with a small gold hoop hanging rakishly from his left ear lobe. Gail from Coronation Street is here, sitting behind us, but Geordie doesn't clock her; he's too busy drawing a diagram in my notebook to show me the process by which silage is supplied to his cows in winter. "That's the feed passage," he says. "Then there's tombstones doon each side like this. They just put their heid in between and drop it doon. They canna actually pull back unless they lift their heid up, so therefore they no take feed back into the … " The rest is drowned out by a table of young men next door. Geordie is, I will discover over the course of two days, only really voluble when the conversation turns to farming, and to his island home of Westray.

Tonight, at least, he has an excuse. He's tired. He left Westray (pop 560) at 9am on a boat for Orkney Mainland, flew to Edinburgh, changed planes and landed at Heathrow at 8pm. This is his first trip to London, and only the sixth time he has been on the British mainland. He's been to Aberdeen and Dundee to see his son play rugby for Orkney; he's been on a canal holiday with his wife, near Inverness; he went to Aviemore once, on "a fact-finding mission to see rabbit-proof fencing". And now he has come to the Ivy, straight from the airport, on a fact-finding mission to see how celebrities live.

We're off to a good start: as we leave the restaurant, our pre-positioned Guardian photographer crosses the road to take Geordie's picture. Two more paparazzi, afraid that they might be missing out on something, rush over to join in. In the frenzy of flashbulbs that follows, Gail from Coronation Street manages to get into her taxi unmolested.

Strolling through the West End toward Piccadilly Circus, Geordie looks far from impressed with the capital by night. "Don't like toons," he says. "Don't like trees, don't like toons, don't like tourists." His mobile rings. It's his wife, Maggie. "Yup," he answers. "Piccadilly Circus, I'm in Piccadilly Circus." He tells her about the paparazzi, and about Gail. "Next time I come down here," he says, "I'm that famous I'll have to get a minder."

The next morning we meet up in Geordie's white-on-white room in the minimalist Hempel hotel in Bayswater. A copy of Orkney Today lies on the wicker coffee table. "Amid Uncertainty Dentist Says Gap Will Be Filled," screams the headline. In the taxi Geordie will not be drawn on the subject of London. "I don't know, it's interestin'," he says. The conversation turns to the subject of cattle. Geordie has about 70 breeding cows, hybrids whose calves are sold for meat marketed as Orkney Gold. It's a tight-run thing, which relies on a 95 per cent pregnancy rate, with almost a quarter of the offspring going to replace existing breeding stock. "The dominant bull is the Charolais," he says. "But you don't keep breeders off the Charolais bull, that's all sold. You're keepin' breeders off your Simmentals and Shorthorn Aberdeen-Angus. That would be your replacements." It is not, apparently, as simple as all that. "You might get a bull that's a tremendous bull, but his heifers have no milk. And you only find out aboot three yair doon the line." I'm nodding sagely. "Do you no have trouble wi' me accent?" he asks.

"No, it's not too bad," I say, recalling a conversation from the previous evening when he told me about some friends of his who had started up a peg firm. I didn't like to ask whether "peg" was an acronym denoting some new chemical process or petroleum by-product, or whether they were just selling pegs, so I played along, figuring I would divine the answer as the story went on. Eventually, I got it: pig farm.

We arrive at Dunhill's of Jermyn Street for Geordie's 11am appointment: a haircut, shave and manicure at the groovy Pankhurst barber shop upstairs. Books about Michael Caine and Hunter S Thompson adorn the shelves. The Italian Job is playing silently on a flatscreen television.

"I think it needs a bit of shape, a bit of structure," says Simon, the barber, but Geordie seems preoccupied with the barber's chair. "I keep thinkin' I should have a pair of six-guns in case the baddies burst in," he says, smiling. Don't they have a barber's chair at the hairdresser's on Westray? "No, it's just an ordinary chair in a wooden hut."

Afterwards, we head to the Vogue Cafe underneath Vogue House for lunch. I have it in mind to introduce Geordie to wheatgrass juice, but they don't have any, so he has to settle for apple, carrot and ginger, which fails to faze him in the slightest. His mobile rings. It's Maggie.

"Hello, Margaret. We're outside Vogue. No, I'm no buyin' anythin', cause there's no prices on anythin' … Yes, fine. I've had a haircut, shave. Fingers is all done up." Their conversation quickly turns to veterinary matters.

I take him to see Trafalgar Square, the gates of Downing Street, the Houses of Parliament. He expends single pictures from his disposable camera on each, for Maggie to see. In the taxi on the way back to the hotel, his judgment is blunt. "It's just a whole lotta buildings, a whole lotta traffic," he says. "I dinna wanna live here, that's for sure. The celebrities can keep it." He pauses, and looks out at the Albert Memorial. "The shave was good." Does he see no point in London at all? "We need London to blame for everything that's gone wrong in the country," he says.

I pick Geordie up for dinner at about 7.30pm. He is wearing a pin-striped suit and a striped tie, which says "Orkney Gold" on it. We are going to Sketch, famed as one of London's most expensive restaurants, although its downstairs Gallery dining room, where we're going, is slightly less prohibitive than the Library upstairs. For some reason, however, the sommelier makes a point of bringing us the upstairs wine list. I think it's because Geordie, freshly shaved and coiffed, is beginning to exude some kind of nascent celebrity. He looks famous. I show him a bottle of wine priced at £4,900. For the first time since he's been in London, his eyes bug out obligingly.

Farmer Geordie's reservations about the celebrity lifestyle do not extend to fine restaurants. He has a big appetite and an adventurous palate, and had not a bad word to say about the food at the Ivy. Neither does he balk tonight, when his lobster salad starter contains exotic fruit and comes in a martini glass, although he does eventually grab the waiter to ask why the martini glass is sitting in a three-inch deep drift of fine brown breadcrumbs. "It's for stability," says the waiter.

Over wine we discuss life on Westray, which is not without its tribulations. The current ferry timetable means that it's impossible for folk to commute to Orkney Mainland for work, although people can, and do, commute the other way round. Every year, young people leave the island, some never to return. "The biggest export from Westray is 16-year-olds," says Geordie. "If you're gonna go away to get educated, what are you gonna come back for?" His half a quail arrives. My veal comes. I pour him another glass of reasonably priced wine. "Tim," he says, "we could get used to this."

After coffee and a selection of fine cheese – Geordie is, by his own admission, "daft on cheese" – we head off to Chinawhite, the sort of nightclub where we might expect to find a few recently sacked soap stars. Almost immediately we realise our mistake. We are neither of us young or stupid enough to enjoy paying £20 each for access to a loud, overcrowded basement where all the chairs are reserved for people who haven't shown up yet, on the offchance that we might get jostled by Dean Gaffney later on. It is, as Geordie puts it, "just a whole load of folk bangin' into each other". In the din it's impossible to explain to him why such places exist, that they essentially serve a moneyed, post-pub crowd suffering from impaired decision-making skills as regards what to do next. They're kebab shops for the rich. "This is bollocks," he shouts in my ear. "This is not real. This is artificial." I look around. If only it weren't real. We make the best of three rounds of drinks, and then return to the Hempel to drain his minibar.

This week on The Farm, Stan Collymore and Debbie McGee tried to milk a cow, and ended up with a bucket full of piss.

Geordie will not have seen this edifying episode; Channel 5 is among the many modern wonders they manage to rub along without on Westray. But everyone on Westray has heard about Geordie's trip to London. When he first got back he walked into his local pub, and someone turned to him and said: "I dinna think you'd be comin' into places like this now you're a celebrity." This week he's back on his farm, making the buildings ready for the cows to wait out the winter and spreading slurry when the gales permit it. He did send me an email, including his final thoughts on his recent and singular brush with fame: "Hope you are well. I am knackered but enjoyed my experience. Rich people are demanding, spoilt, arrogant, artificial and sad. Nightclub was shite. Geordie Drever."

Dog's Dinner

The good news is, a New Zealand woman is offering to ship 42 tonnes of food aid to famine-hit Kenya. The bad news is she wants to send dog food. The good news is that the woman, pet-food manufacturer Christine Drummond, claims her dog food is a delicious and healthy mixture of freeze-dried pork, beef, mussels, deer velvet (ie antler) and flax seed, which she eats herself and feeds to her children. The bad news is that the Kenyan special programmes minister, John Munyes, described the offer as immoral, unacceptable, offensive and demeaning. Thereafter the main elements of this story become more friable. Drummond has said that the mix she intended to send was not really dog food – although it's made from the same stuff – but a nutritional supplement specially designed for people. A Kenyan government spokesman nevertheless called the offer "naive and culturally insulting given the meaning of dogs in our culture". You wouldn't want to choose sides at this point.

However, one major question remains: is it OK to eat dog food or not? Unless I lose my nerve, I am about to find out. To my profound disappointment, there is nothing on the label of the dog food I give my dog about it being unfit for humans. There is a reference to its "superb taste", although I'm not sure how anyone knows this. According to Nicole Harrison of the Pet Food Manufacturers Association, the meat in pet food must by law come from animals fit for human consumption. But does that mean it's fine for me to eat it? "Absolutely," says Harrison. "I mean, obviously, it's not advisable to eat dog food as a major part of your diet." Don't you worry.

The flavour I have chosen is called, rather cryptically, "With Lamb in Jelly". What with lamb in jelly? On the plate it looks the same as any other dog food, its presentation unimproved by the fine china or the sprig of parsley. I thought I'd got used to the smell of the stuff over the years, but it takes on a whole new unpleasantness when accompanied by the imminent prospect of putting some in your mouth.

If you extrapolate from the chart on the label, an adult dog my weight would need to eat more than seven tins of the stuff a day (depending on how active he is) to stay healthy. I believe a mouthful, maybe less, will be enough to get the idea. Unfortunately, I have two children at home with the flu, and they have leapt from their sick beds to see Daddy eat dog food. I bring a forkful to my lips; it's closer than my face has ever been to dog food. In it goes.

The taste, I have to say, is curiously bland, if nonetheless insistent: a musty, slightly fishy tang which I would characterise as some way off superb. The texture, however, is truly horrible – slippery and reconstituted, as if it has been predigested. It is virtually impossible to overcome my reluctance to swallow it, although some goes down by accident. The children shriek with delight. I give the rest to the dog, with none of the usual sense that I am doing her a giant favour.

Don't Get Shirty With Me

"I disapprove of what you say, but I will defend to the death your right to say it," is a deeply unsatisfactory quotation for several reasons. First, while it's attributed to Voltaire, he never actually said it. Second, no one really feels this way. Personally I wouldn't skip lunch in order to defend someone's right to say something I disagreed with. Third, it doesn't make an exception for people who choose to express themselves using a T-shirt.

In America there is some question as to whether T-shirt slogans constitute protected free speech, but I am happy to side-step this issue because I see nothing wrong with having one law for T-shirt wearers and another for the rest of us. Even if I approve of what your T-shirt says I would, were it in my gift, deny you the right to wear it. I don't care if Jesus is Your Homeboy. I don't care which member of your family went where and then failed to bring you anything back other than an item of apparel which revels in its own lousiness. I don't care if You Only Drink to Make Me Interesting. Because your T-shirt has asked me to, I am now expressly not going to Make Poverty History.

Along with the bumper sticker, the slogan-bearing T-shirt is the preserve of that group of people who believe you can buy wit, spiritual profundity or principle from a shop at the far corner of a mall. Even funny T-shirts are at their most hilarious while they're on the rail. Any residual wit evaporates once you put it on and go outside in it. Amusement-wise, it's the equivalent of walking down the road shouting the same joke over and over. And if it's on a T-shirt, chances are most people have heard it by now.

The latest sartorial controversy surrounds the popularity of Stop Snitchin' T-shirts in the States, perhaps the first fashion item designed with the intimidation of material witnesses in mind. Several trials have been disrupted by spectators turning up wearing Stop Snitchin' shirts with the clear intention of silencing those testifying, and the mayor of Boston has now threatened to ban them. The American Civil Liberties Union, meanwhile, is trying to stop him. But it's not only the witness intimidators who fancy themselves in these things. It is, like the I'm So Happy I Could Just Shit shirts of yesteryear, a must-have bit of wardrobe for every idiot with a torso. The Baltimore Sun recently interviewed a guy who was buying one, and he denied being anti-snitch in any way. "I just like the shirt," he said. "It's just a figure of speech." Then he said: "I work at a car rental company."

Here, then, is the problem: is the guy in the front row wearing a Stop Snitchin' shirt in order to pervert the course of justice, or is he wearing it because his No Fat Chicks shirt is in the wash? The ACLU is now in the unenviable position of defending to the death the right to wear a T-shirt that makes you look a witless, uncomprehending prat. I know that's part of their Voltarian mission, but if it were up to me we would incinerate every last … ooh, hang on – lunch.

Ben & Jerry's: The Next Wave

The ice cream brand Ben & Jerry's has been forced to apologise to its Irish customers after releasing a new flavour dubbed Black

& Tan. In its defence, the American company claimed that the ice cream had been named in honour of the classic mixture of stout and pale ale, and not the notorious 8,000-strong British irregular force that arrived in Ireland in 1920 and is remembered chiefly for its habit of firing indiscriminately on crowds of civilians.

"We were not aware of that," said a spokesman for Ben & Jerry's. It's an easy mistake to make.

Fortunately, the company has a whole raft of new flavours scheduled for release next year. Here's a sample from its latest European product launch:

- **Orange March Sorbet** "Pure sorbet made with fresh oranges from Florida's early March harvest. What?"
- **Chocolate Exorcism** "Fudge-injected, treble-chocolate ice cream with dark chocolate sauce, forcibly encrusted with chocolate. One taste of this and you will feel like calling in a priest! Don't laugh, it's happened."
- **Guantánamo Surprise** "What's in it? That's top secret. Our specially selected panel of tasters were blindfolded, flown to a secret location and force-fed the stuff, and they still couldn't guess what was in it – even when we told them exactly what to say over and over."
- **Ginger Binge** "A great-tasting way to reward yourself for any sudden, dramatic weight loss."
- **Spearmint Rhino** "Don't worry: there's no rhino in it! In fact,

10p from every tub sold goes to a rhinoceros reserve in Africa. And the spearmint is organic."

- **Summer Fruit Tsunami** "Sorry. That one shouldn't be in there. Our mistake."
- **Delhi Belhi** "Enjoy a 'Belhi-full' of this delicious cinnamon and cardamom-infused ice cream. Get it?"
- **Mouthful O' Shaved Nuts** "This one contains fresh slivered almonds and was a big favourite stateside, but we're delaying its international release due to a pending copyright issue. Apparently, there's some movie with the same name."
- **Vanilla Parker Bowles** "Our best vanilla, packaged in a special-edition tub designed to commemorate the reign of everybody's favourite queen."
- **Londonderry Berry** "Brand new, mixed-berry frozen yoghurt named in honour of Ireland's capital. Sorry?"

Rights & Responsibilities

Welcome to the NewsRoom at permachat.co.uk, the UK's premiere online current affairs forum!

>connecting to server ...

Current Host: Chris2:

Current Topic: The prime minister has launched what he calls "a conversation with the nation", a consultation with voters about the problems facing the government. Is this a genuine attempt to re-engage the public, or a PR gimmick? What do you think?

Pashmina: rachel steven's boyfreind is unhappy with her sexy new image

Bronco: who he

Host_Chris2: well how do you feel abt the issues raised by the Queen's speech on Wednesday?

LadeezMan: dunno wot r they

Pashmina: jeremy edwards of holby city fame

Host_Chris2: for example: do you think gay people should be allowed to marry?

Bronco: oh

LadeezMan: yes but only if they can prove they have changed

Pashmina: the couple are back together after a brief spilt

Host_Chris2: no, I mean marry other gay people

Pashmina: LadeezMan you cant change from being gay!!!!!

Bronco: no matter how hard u try

LadeezMan: shutup

Pashmina: its something ur born with, like weak enamel!!!

Host_Chris2: the issue is the protection in law accorded to married couples

Bronco: hows yr teeth btw

Pashmina: got 2 hav 2 corwns

Bronco: wot

Pashmina: crowns even

LadeezMan: expansive

Host_Chris2: we're straying a bit here

capitalistpiglet has entered the NewsRoom

capitalistpiglet: hi room

Pashmina: hi piglet

capitalistpiglet: how was the dentist

Pashmina: i got weak enamle

LadeezMan: u shoud of flossed more

Pashmina: I WAS BORN WITH IT. ITS GENETIC

Host_Chris2: let's return to the topic people

Bronco: piglet do you think gays shoud be allowed to marry

LadeezMan: other gays

capitalistpiglet: of course

LadeezMan: r u gay

Pashmina: dont anser him

capitalistpiglet: no, i'm not

Bronco: not answering or not gay

LadeezMan: im not gay

capitalistpiglet: I just think gay couples deserve the option of legal marital status

Host_Chris2: the very point I was trying to make. Are there any questions?

LadeezMan: yes

Host_Chris2: other than about my sexual preferences

LadeezMan: oh

Pashmina: Chris2 wot do u think abt Rachel Steven's sexy new look

Host_Chris2: I really don't care one way or another

LadeezMan: thought so

>connection to server has been terminated...

My Vision for a British Bill of Rights

We need, says the Tory leader, David Cameron, a "British bill of rights" – one that isn't quite so overrun with rights as the Human Rights Act. Instead it would enshrine rights that are peculiarly British in character, such as the Right to As Many Trials By Jury As It Takes to Secure a Conviction. This "commonsense" alternative would also "spell out the fundamental duties and responsibilities of people living in this country", which makes it sound more like a list of chores. But the idea that rights are concomitant with responsibilities is steadily gaining popularity. Below are a few of the basic human obligations currently vying for inclusion in the bill:

- **The Responsibility to Remain Silent** This would mainly apply to young people, especially the ones hanging around outside shops, but also to cinema-goers, rail passengers, library-users and anyone who hinders the fight against terrorism by going on and on about how much it hurts to be accidentally shot by the police.

- **The Responsibility to Shoot Intruders** "Intruders", in this case, means anyone who is in your house who should not be there (or, if you are the police, anyone who is in a house). Obviously this definition requires judicious interpretation – it doesn't apply to the babysitter's boyfriend, for example. Although one less babysitter's boyfriend in the world isn't going to cause too much hand-wringing, and in the end it's your word against hers. Just use your common sense.

- **The Responsibility to Give Politicians the Benefit of the Doubt** The British people should not criticise every single minor mistake made by politicians. That is the job of other politicians.

- **The Responsibility to Look Innocent** It used to be held that if you had nothing to hide you had nothing to fear, but in these challenging times unfounded suspicions are sometimes all the police have to go on. British citizens – and foreign nationals, and tourists – have a duty to dress smartly and act as if they have a legitimate reason to be where they are. In fact, it would be easier if we all just went round with our hands in the air.

- **The Responsibility to Leave the Country When It Becomes Apparent That You Are No Longer Wanted** When a cricketer is dismissed he does not sit sullenly in a detention centre awaiting a verdict from some court in Strasbourg. He takes his bat and he walks. This is the British way, although it doesn't apply to British people because they don't have anywhere else to go.

- **The Responsibility to Behave With the Utmost Decency At All Times** It's hard to define decency, but we all know what it isn't: it isn't swearing on the bus or having a dangerous dog or coming out of prison well before you've finished your whole sentence. With responsibilities like these, who needs rights? Let common sense prevail!

Welcome to the NewsRoom at permachat.co.uk, the UK's premier online current affairs forum!

>connecting to server...
Current Host: Chris2

Current Topic: The case of whistleblower Katharine Gun has highlighted government fears about the legality of the Iraq war and shows that America was prepared to use espionage in an attempt to obtain a second UN resolution. But was Gun right to leak the information? What do you think?

Pashmina: but if its givin people work stress then u can sack them

Host_Chris2: I'm not sure I understand

Pashmina: if the noise is annoyin everyl

LadeezMan has entered the NewsRoom

Host_Chris2: it's just an expression. you don't actually blow a whistle.

nameless: SPYING IS ESSENTIAL TO OUR SECURITY

LadeezMan: hi room

Pashmina: hi LadeezMan were was u last week

LadeezMan: I got a job

Pashmina: ooh! How is it!

Host_Chris2: welcome back LadeezMan.

LadeezMan: was. I got the sack.

Host_Chris2: I trust it wasn't for blowing the whistle on illegal intelligence activity!

nameless: OR TREASON FOR SHORT

LadeezMan: no stealing

Pashmina: its not a real whislte tho

GCHQop4: I'm in

Pashmina: you can if it is abt war becos war is wrong

GCHQrec1: bingo. receiving

LadeezMan: wot abt world war 2 tho

Pashmina: they didnt no any better back then.

Bronco has entered the NewsRoom

Pashmina: hi bronco

GCHQop4: run "Bronco"

Bronco: hi

GCHQrec1: sending from 18A Langley Terrace Bristol BS3 0JS

Bronco: how u know my address

GCHQop4: copy. A few anti-cap marches, nothing major

Pashmina: who r they

GCHQop4: run "Pashmina"

GCHQrec1: Bracknell Road, Chester

Pashmina: hey!!!!

GCHQop4: fined for affray 04/2001

LadeezMan: wikkid

Pashmina: i didnt start it!

GCHQop4: should what we're typing be appearing on the screen

Host_Chris2: let's stick to the topic, people: whistleblowing

GCHQrec1: shit. Abort

GCHQop4 has left the NewsRoom

GCHQrec1 has left the NewsRoom

nameless: KEEP UP THE GOOD WORK BOYS

>connection to server has been terminated...

It's Time to Take Sides

I feel the time has come for me to join the forces currently waging what the Daily Mail likes to call the "war on motorists". In the Mail's estimation, the anti-motoring forces are winning – recently, through their subsidiaries the Avon & Somerset police, they managed to fine some hapless road user for driving through a puddle – and I'm ready to jump on their bandwagon.

Where do I sign up? There doesn't seem to be an official recruiting body. If the government is coordinating this assault on the Great British Driver, shouldn't they at least have a website where I can buy a "Driving Sucks" T-shirt?

The pro-motorist forces have lots of websites. On the Association of British Drivers page you can buy golf umbrellas bearing the ABD logo ("Great for outdoor events!"), but I could not locate the corresponding brolly for the nanny-state anti-motorist brigade ("Warning: unsuitable for indoor events").

The ABD website makes mention of a "powerful and vociferous minority of people, backed by much of the media, and wilfully exploited by government", whose aim is "to persuade you that your car is bad for your health", but it doesn't give a phone number for them. The organisations most frequently cited for being anti-motorist, such as Friends of the Earth and Transport 2000, seem to me to be busy with all sorts of extraneous political agendas. I don't care about global warming or integrated transport solutions. I just hate motorists. I want to make everything bad for them. I want to see less parking, higher petrol prices, more speed cameras and road charging to fund the eventual elimination of roads. Where will you drive then, Mr Motorist? On the towpath?

I was initially unsure whether I even qualified to fight the war against the motorist, because I am technically a motorist, although it's not exactly how I wish to be remembered. It's like going about billing yourself as a "taxpayer" or a "shopper". Call me ambitious, but I'd much rather be captioned "Tim Dowling, hammer of British drivers" than "Tim Dowling, motorist", even if the latter is more accurate.

I'm also in the RAC, although the only part of their evil pro-motorist agenda I agree with is the bit where they come and pick me up off the hard shoulder. This still struck me as possibly a tiny bit hypocritical, until I noticed that one of the ABD members profiled on their website makes the rather smug point that he is also a pedestrian. If he can walk and belong to a group that calls itself "the voice of the driver" at the same time, then surely I can wage war on motorists from within the RAC.

In fact I'm ideally poised to work as a sort of double agent, chiefly by getting out there and giving motorists a bad name. My specialty is inconsiderate driving, coincidentally the very offence the abovementioned puddle-rusher was done for. Only the other day someone was so astounded by my lack of vehicular grace that he was moved to spit on my car. Cyclists: the next time I cut you up, remember – I'm doing this for us.

The Wettest Drought Yet

Not being native to these isles, I used to have trouble under-standing what people meant by the word drought. "It's terribly worrying, isn't it, the drought?" they would say. Perhaps, I thought to myself, they're talking about some obscure livestock ailment, or maybe they just pronounce "draft" funny. But I know they can't be talking about that other thing, the not having enough water thing, because it's raining frigging sideways.

Even today when people say, "It's been so dry these past two winters, hasn't it?", I nod in vague agreement, but I think, "What are you talking about? Compared with where?" This week, hosepipe bans came into effect across the south-east, making it illegal for 10 million people to water their gardens or wash their cars with a hose. I have more or less accepted that England is a country where adequate water supplies are main-tained only through unrelenting, round-the-clock rain, and that any gap in the clouds spells doom, followed by standpipes in the streets. I also know it's no use pointing out that it's rain-ing right now. I know it's the wrong kind of rain. It's too wet, or something.

This is nevertheless my first official hosepipe ban, and in a panic at the prospect of it I rushed out and spent a hundred quid on a giant water butt made out of an old whisky barrel. After I installed it I got a bit worried because I read that if you let a barrel dry out it will collapse into a pile of staves and hoops. Even my precaution seemed like a form of moronic optimism. Why didn't I just get the ugly green plastic kind of water butt? Didn't I realise there was a drought on?

Well here it is, the first week in April, and my barrel runneth over. The lid is floating on its brimming surface. I've got more water than I know what to do with, presuming I can attach a hose to my barrel without breaking the law. But I still have many questions about the details of the ban. For example, can I wash my car with the water that flows under its wheels from the broken main up the road? It's been running like a babbling brook all winter, excepting the day the men from Thames Water came to fix it, when it exploded like a geyser and shot mud and gravel into the neighbour's open third-storey window, after which the men ran away. Sometimes I think it would be nice to have a standpipe instead, so we could at least turn it off.

This is of course just a small part of the 915,000 litres a day – 17 Olympic swimming pools an hour – that Thames Water loses through leaks, representing a third of the total supply. They say they're currently spending £500,000 a day repairing London's network of 150-year-old Victorian pipes, but I am not very impressed with them leaving it so long. I blame their complacency on the relative harmlessness of water. You don't see the gas people letting a third of their product leak away in transit. If you want any water this summer, see me. I'll be giving it away, and mine tastes faintly of whisky.

PermaBlog – Non-stop comment for a non-stop planet!

Saving the Planet Doesn't Make Financial Sense

The basic flaws in both Brown's and Cameron's proposals are the figures. The targets set are both burdensome and economically unrealistic, and yet they will achieve nothing ... *[read more]*

Posted by DrKarlMaglev at 0926 today

Dr Karl Maglev holds the Halliburton chair in Advanced Climatonomics at Philip Morris University

COMMENTS

So basically, Dr Maglev, you're now saying that global warming – which you denied for years – cannot be reversed. How convenient.

SixKindsOfChris at 0954 today

I'm not saying it can't be reversed. I'm saying that given the price tag, it doesn't make sense to bother.

DrKarlMaglev at 1010 today

How can it not make sense????!!!!!! Hi Chris

JaneT at 1014 today

Believe me, if you understood the figures, you'd realise that it's more cost effective to let the Earth die

SixKindsOfChris at 1017 today

I agree. There's no way we can cut our greenhouse gas emissions by 60 per cent. We can't afford it.

liberati at 1031 today

At last, someone who understands basic climatonomics.

DrKarlMaglev at 1039 today

Great. Except I was being sarcastic. We can reduce the CO_2 in our atmosphere if we cut our energy use drastically.

SixKindsOfChris at 1044 today

I did try switching to energy-saving light bulbs, but they make you look AWFUL. The politicians don't tell you that.

JaneT at 1048 today

I'm so glad someone else said that.

TammyFlu at 1056 today

Is that what it comes down to? The planet's existence hangs in the balance because people don't like they way they look in energy efficient light?

SixKindsOfChris at 1100 today

If you had one above your bathroom mirror, you'd never leave the house!
JaneT at 1107 today

It's pointless – carbon trading, light bulbs, insulation – none of this is going to be anything like enough to stop global warming. Shouldn't we be looking for another planet?
liberati at 1113 today

"Global Warming" is a myth designed to justify Ken Livingstone's evil congestion charge. My school run is in disarray, and now the French antique garden furniture shop on the high street is closing. What will it take, people?
LauraW at 1117 today

Question – My electric car caught fire. How many trees should I plant?
ElSmell at 1136 today

We must lower the tax on contaminated petrol
liberati at 1141 today

Relax – global warming is all part of Satan's plan.
MegaDave at 1149 today

I was thinking of joining forces with Satan, so I could get one

of those patio heaters without feeling guilty. Do you have any literature, MegaDave?

liberati at 1157 today

I don't think you people are taking my points seriously. We cannot stop global warming by making it illegal to leave your TV on standby.

DrKarlMaglev at 1201 today

Check out my website: www.davesworldofpain.co.uk. You can download all the forms.

MegaDave at 1212 today

I can think of some people I'd like to put on standby, namely Ken bloody Livingstone.

LauraW at 1218 today

I can think of some people I'd like to switch off at the wall.

JaneT at 1220 today

You must be registered to post a comment

HOV Negative

Welcome to the car-pool lane. You may have seen one like it while travelling the highways of America – a special lane with white diamonds painted on it, for the exclusive use of drivers with inflatable sex dolls in their passenger seats. Construction of Britain's first car-pool lane – along a busy 10-mile section of the M1 – begins next week.

In the America of my youth, car-pooling (the verb form dates back to 1962, so don't blame me for degrading the language; it was like that when I got here) was a word to describe me being driven home from swimming lessons by someone else's mother, or groups of parsimonious commuters travelling from the same suburb to the same city in the same car. It was based on the old-fashioned idea that driving was neither a right nor a privilege but a loathsome and costly chore. As far back as the Arab oil embargo of the 70s, the powers that be decided to coopt this grassroots solution by rewarding car-poolers, and punishing everyone else.

So the HOV lane was born. HOV stands for high-occupancy vehicle, although in California two people riding in a nine-seat SUV is considered high occupancy. The choice of lanes left drivers with a dilemma: is the main object of a successful car journey to arrive at one's destination on time, or to be alone in the car for two hours so you can eat 11 Mars bars while indulging a devotion to Lite FM?

Over the years Americans have exercised considerable ingenuity in order to enjoy life in the fast lane. In the DC area there are established "slug lines" where commuters queue up to wait for drivers in search of an occupant, and this in a country where the Hitchhiking Psychopath is the national bogeyman. The right of the unborn child to be considered a fully fledged passenger has been argued by pregnant women, without, it has to be said, much success. It's unclear whether a dead person counts. What if he was alive when you set off?

Recently a Denver man caught travelling with a mannequin in his front seat was sentenced to spend four one-hour sessions standing by the highway holding a sign that says "HOV Not for Dummies". When it comes to car-pooling, even the justice system has been forced to innovate.

Car-pool lanes have wrought so many profound changes in American life that it's easier to enumerate the things they don't do, such as: they don't reduce traffic congestion. This is unfortunate, not least because it's precisely why they're being introduced to Britain, but it's obvious when you think about it: the reason the car-pool lane is the equivalent of a long, thin VIP room is because it doesn't have very many cars in it. In terms of traffic through-put, it doesn't pull its weight. In the States they've already begun to open them up to hybrid car owners and lone drivers willing to pay a toll, which is basically the beginning of the end.

But never mind about all that. Welcome aboard. I don't have room for my car pool-tunnel syndrome joke, but it's really just a punchline in search of a set-up, so I leave it with you in flat-pack form.

PermaBlog – Non-stop comment for a non-stop planet!

English Is The Key

As a nation we cannot provide equal opportunity without first providing basic skills. Ethnic minorities earn on average a third less than other workers, and a poor grasp of English has been identified as a major factor in this discrepancy. We owe it to the 40,000 non-English speakers currently who are being denied employment to … *[read more]*

Posted by Trenda Contently at 1007 today

Trenda Contently is the author of Holy Alimony and It's Raining Jerks! She is also a prospective Tory candidate for Glasgow North.

COMMENTS

…to kick them off the welfare rolls forthwith.

SixKindsOfChris at 1022 today

This is Labour policy. Why would a prospective Tory candidate choose to wrap herself in the opposition's clothing?

liberati at 1040 today

I think I've answered my own question there.
liberati at 1046 today

What we're talking about is getting people into language classes so that they can take advantage of the employment opportunities that are out there. And yes, we'd need to incentivise that option, ultimately with the threat of losing benefit.
TrendaC at 1051 today

The government is posing this very same threat, with the added twist that they're cutting provision for free access to English tuition at the same time. How are you going to outflank that?
SixKindsOfChris at 1059 today

---

simpel – no lern the engilsh, no get the money
SE14 at 1102 today

HAPPY VALENTINES DAY EVERYONE (Hi Chris!)
JaneT at 1113 today

Hi JaneT. Thank you for the virtual chocolates
SixKindsOfChris at 1126 today

You're welcome. Did you get the pic I emailed? I was worried your spam filter might block it because it shows so much skin.
JaneT at 1131 today

I admire your forthrightness, SE14

TrendaC at 1139 today

Wot I dont understond u

SE14 at 1152 today

You put things very succinctly. Where are you from?

TrendaC at 1202 today

SE14

SE14 at 1204 today

The English can barely speak English. Is the government going to punish people for poor grammar?

ElSmell at 1217 today

---

that I would vote for

liberati at 1219 today

No, SE14 – I mean where are you from originally?

TrendaC at 1225 today

Oh. Devon.

SE14 at 1229 today

I didn't get the job at Starbucks because my Polish wasn't good enough. Dzięki oprócz nie dzięki!

MegaDave at 1232 today

We cannot continue to let foreign speakers dominate and destroy our British way of life.

TrendaC at 1247

That is a totally racsist thing to say!

JaneT at 1253 today

Is it? I thought it meant "thanks but no thanks". I told you my Polish sucks.

MegaDave at 1257 today

Not you! TrendaC you'd be better off as a candidate for the BNP!

JaneT at 1301 today

I know, but of course they went with a bloke in the end. Men!

TrendaC at 1306 today

You must be registered to post a comment

Crime & Punishment

My Sangatte Hell

Every night they gather at sunset near the bent wire gate of Sangatte's Red Cross refugee camp. Dressed in dusty jackets, torn scarves, old blankets and hoods that obscure their faces, these so-called asylum seekers smoke cigarettes and chat quietly about Stephen Byers' resignation. Soon they will walk the well-worn path that links the camp with the nearby Frethun marshalling yards, where freight trains begin their journey through the Channel tunnel. Tonight I will go with them.

They all have their own reasons for wanting to enter the UK illegally. One, a bearded young man with eyes that reminded one of the Express's Yvonne Ridley, said he was doing a series of features on the camp. Another showed me a false Iraqi passport and an expired NUJ card. He needed a quick 2,000 words to fulfil his contract with a well-known broadsheet and was hoping to get bitten by a guard dog. A balding cameraman in a Voodoo Lounge T-shirt told me he had come to Sangatte only the day before with GMTV's Lara Logan. He pointed her out to me. She was wearing a baseball cap and a Spider-Man mask, but she still looked beautiful.

French police estimate that as many as two dozen British journalists now attempt the perilous journey through the Channel tunnel every night. They cannot catch them all, and even those they manage to stop are unrepentant, returning night after night in pursuit of a news feature or a few minutes on From Our Own Correspondent.

At 9pm we make our way to Frethun, carrying with us nothing but the clothes on our backs, our notebooks, our mobiles, our laptops, tape recorders, extra pens, personal organisers, 200 duty-free Silk Cut and in some cases, make-up and portable lighting equipment. By midnight, seven of us have evaded the gendarmes patrolling the perimeter fence. Once inside we split up. It helps to follow the genuine asylum seekers, but it's not always easy to tell who's who in the dark. Mistakes are inevitable. Last month a Mirror reporter clung to the wrong train and ended up in Disneyland Paris. I asked him about Space Mountain. He said it was cool.

In the end I was not one of the lucky ones. I got into an argument with a freelance who kept helping himself to my Hob Nobs, and the noise brought the gendarmes running. We were both dragged to a collection point and put on a bus back to Sangatte. It seemed I would not, after all, be travelling to Kent, where I had rather foolishly left my car parked on a double yellow. But I will try again tomorrow. I will keep trying until I succeed. The editor says there might be some space on Thursday. Until then, this will have to do.

A Letter from the News of the World

Dear Prostitute,

You don't know me, but I am a journalist working at the News of the World. No doubt you are aware of our newspaper's commitment to hard-hitting investigative journalism. We did that paedophile thing, remember? You may not be aware that we also remain committed to soft-hitting investigative journalism. That's why we need your help.

Do you ever encounter celebrities in the course of your business? What about TV presenters, professional sportsmen, Radio 1 DJs or minor royals? If so, we want to hear from you. We're interested in information on the sex lives of virtually every type of celebrity (not journalists), and like your customers, we're willing to pay for it.

At the NOTW we have only the greatest respect for the work you do, which is why we know you will want to help us expose the slimy love rats who betray their wives by paying for sex with cheap tarts. Like that Angus Deayton, for example. Or Jamie Theakston, except he was single.

You may be asking yourself, why should I take my story to the NOTW? At the risk of sounding boastful, this paper has an outstanding record of paying prostitutes for information. Here is what you will get:

- Three nights in a five-star hotel of your choice, while you are grilled by our sleaze desk reporters.
- Your story told in a national Sunday newspaper with a circulation of around 4m. You will become a celebrity prostitute overnight. Many of our most successful actresses began their careers as women of easy virtue.
- Payment commensurate with the name-recognition value of the celebrity you have slept with. A current tariff is available from the news desk.
- A reputation certain to boost your earning power should you decide to return to your former life as a common streetwalker.

Don't worry about your steamy celebrity sex sessions being confidential. They aren't, and we've been to court to prove it. Of course, the NOTW complies fully with all the guidelines regarding the investigation of celebrity sex secrets as laid out by the PCC and its acting chairman, Robert Pinker. Please let us know if you have ever had sex with this man.

You will need to keep detailed notes of your encounters, paying special attention to perverted requests, arrogant claims, admissions of illegal acts, as well as any distinctive and/or amusing physical characteristics. Remember: we cannot pay you if you become a witness in a police investigation, so no talking to the rozzers.

You will find my business card attached. We hope you will consider working with us, but if you decide not to, please keep the throwaway camera as our free gift.

Welcome to the NewsRoom at permachat.co.uk, the UK's premier online current affairs forum!

>connecting to server...

Current Host: Chris2

Current Topic: According to the British Crime Survey violent crime rose by an alarming 11 per cent in the second quarter of 2004, even as overall crime fell by 5 per cent. Is Britain becoming a more violent society? What do you think?

nameless: THE ANSWER IS SIMPLE: MORE PRISONS

Host_Chris2: but does prison work?

capitalistpiglet: I think most of the increase is down to low-level thuggery

nameless: WE NEED TO FIGHT VIOLENCE WITH VIOLENCE

Bronco: sounds cool

Pashmina has entered the NewsRoom

capitalistpiglet: & an increasing willingness to report minor offences

Pashmina: yo room

Bronco: hi pash

Host_Chris2: that's an interesting point – has anyone had recent experience of violent crime?

Pashmina: I did last weekend

Bronco: where

Pashmina: in a nightclub

capitalistpiglet: was alcohol a factor?

Pashmina: yes

Host_Chris2: are you comfortable sharing it with us?

Pashmina: it was no big deal just a bloody nose & ripped out earring

Host_Chris2: did you report it to the police

Pashmina: no

capitalistpiglet: were you ashamed?

Pashmina: no way. she deserved it

nameless: WE NEED TO CRACK DOWN ANTISOCIAL BEHAVIOUR

Pashmina: amen

Host_Chris2: OK. any other examples?

Pashmina: I bet she say sorry next time she spill somebodys breezer

Bronco: does a wallet stolen off a bar stool count

capitalistpiglet: was there any violence involved in the theft?

Bronco: no. I just took the cards and chucked it in a skip

Host_Chris2: does anyone have an example in which they figure as the victim?

Pashmina: nothing spring to mind

capitalistpiglet: someone called me a wanker on the bus yesterday

nameless: I AM MUGGED ANNUALLY BY THE INLAND REVENUE

Bronco: Its embarising but I got held up by a 8 year old with a pen knife last month

Pashmina: omg that is SOOO cute!!!!!

>connection to server has been terminated…

Thinking Inside the Box

Tuesday, 8pm I arrive at the Guardian's offices to see for the first time the large Perspex "coffin" that has been constructed to my exacting specifications: 7ft by 7ft by 3ft; the same size as the one in which David Blaine will spend 44 days suspended over the Thames. I notice it has no roof, and no door. I briefly wish I had been more exacting, and perhaps a bit more specific, but there is no going back now. One of the walls must be removed and then screwed back into place once I have entered.

The hurried nature of this performance – I don't like the word stunt – means I've had to cut a few corners in order to pip Blaine at the post. By spending only 24 hours in my box, hoisted 3ft in the air by a fork-lift truck behind the Guardian building, I'm not so much copying his ordeal as traducing it. I've tried to grow a Blaine-style mystery goatee, but it feels a bit sparse. Blaine will have fresh water piped in to his box and a catheter to take away his urine. I've just brought a big bottle of water in with me, and my arrangements for the latter contingency are still a bit sketchy when they start sealing me in.

Suddenly the last of a very small band of well-wishers has gone, and I am alone. Alone in a box with nothing but the clothes on my back and enough water to last me 24 hours. And a little mat to sleep on. And a sleeping bag and a pillow. And an extra fleece in case it gets parky. And a mobile phone, for emergencies. And a couple of magazines and some books. And a radio. And some cashews.

10pm The little yard behind the Guardian is unusually bright at night. Two security lights shine directly into my face. Above me, through the open roof of my prison, the sky is flat and sulphurtinged. No stars can pierce London's thick sodium halo. I wonder if birds can get in here. I can't be in a box with a bird.

11.15pm I'm a little confused about what I'm doing, and it strikes me that I should have thought harder about it before getting into the box. In emulating Blaine's latest challenge, am I emulating a feat of endurance, or an illusion? Blaine swears his stunt (I don't mind using the word in this case) is for real, a legitimate experiment in privation, but he's a magician – his word is, by definition, worth nothing. With genuine endurance tests, people expect a bit of independent validation of the authenticity of the proceedings. If it's just a magic trick, then it's impolite to ask how it's done. For me, the distinction has suddenly become important: I need to know if I'm allowed to eat the cashews.

12.08am I don't think I've ever tried to sleep anywhere so noisy. I'm surrounded by giant whirring fans and shuddering duct-work. The hum seems to get louder as the night wears on. Blaine made the right decision when he chose to dangle over the river. At least there he will be able to get a little shuteye.

By coincidence I was in New York when Blaine spent three days in a block of ice. He was only a short walk from my hotel, and I went two or three times to have a look. Over time the little cavity he was in got bigger as the ice melted, but it still looked like a particularly unpleasant form of self-torture: forehead against the ice, gaze vacant, feet shifting. It seems to me that Blaine has scheduled his big stunts the wrong way round: first he was buried alive for a week, then went into the ice, and then he spent 35 hours balanced on an 80ft pillar. You could quibble about the exact order, but it's obvious that being buried alive should come after spending six weeks in a see-through box. The first is terrifying; the second is just inconvenient.

1.20am There is no way I'm ever going to get any sleep with all this noise. How do people live round here?

6.02am I am woken two or three times by sharp pains, which I think might be pressure sores, but it turns out I am sleeping on my keys. At about 5.30am a lorry shows up and unloads the morning newspapers. I manage to doze off again, but at about 10 minutes to six someone starts up a motorbike 3ft from my head. I decide not to try again.

While I sleep, someone leaves the Best Loved Hotel Guide For England and Wales propped up against the Perspex. This is clearly meant to be a joke, but I find it a little creepy. Eventually, the morning security guard arrives, bemused after a week off. "When I left there was a skip here," he says. He changes into his uniform and brings me a cup of coffee.

8.30am Guardian employees begin arriving for work. Some don't seem to notice me, but most give me at least a glance, perhaps a smile. A few approach the box and say things, although I can't always hear them. "What time do they let you out?" is popular, as is "Good luck! Don't drink too much!" The latter is becoming more apposite by the minute. So far I've had a dozen offers of coffee and I've accepted three. I really, really need to urinate. What do I do?

9.12am Ahhhhhh. I don't want to be too specific about how I solved the pee thing. It's not that I'm prudish; I just think a little Blaine-esque mystery might be appropriate here. I will say that by a lucky coincidence a van pulls up and parks directly in front of my box, blocking the view for those coming and going from the building.

11.16am A Guardian employee – one might say "colleague" if that term didn't imply a generally supportive attitude towards the efforts of fellow journalists – leans out of a window and shouts, "Oi! Cut your ear off!" This is an amusing reference to a stunt Blaine pulled at a recent press conference, but I don't find it funny. Here's a warning for Mr Blaine: it may take weeks for your muscles to waste, but the sense of humour is one of the first things to go. Inside the box, nothing is funny.

As it happens I had prepared and practised one of Blaine's tricks, just in case someone demands some magic, of which more later. Don't get your hopes up, by the way.

12.34pm I am lying in my box, reading a New Yorker article about the men who work in the tunnels below Manhattan. I feel a special kinship with these so-called "sandhogs", even though they toil unseen in unspeakable conditions and I have an audience of half a dozen people who are watching me read a magazine.

A bike messenger raps on the glass. When you live in a Perspex cube, there's no pretending you're not at home. "How long you been in there for?" he asks. "Just over 15 hours," I shout. "Why?" "Because David Blaine is doing it." My voice and my answer sound equally hollow. I imagine my mother saying, "If David Blaine jumped off a bridge, would you do that, too?"

1pm Lunch is a pasta salad passed over the wall by a conspirator. It's preferable to allowing my body to cannibalise my own organs for nutrients, but only just. What is it about letting pasta go cold that makes it "salad"? The word has no meaning. I'm losing my grip.

2.10pm I start to doze off while reading, but it's difficult with so many people watching, mostly smokers taking a break out back. Sometimes they offer me fags. No way. Not in the box. Frankly, I'm probably tired enough to sleep through the last stretch, but I feel a strange obligation to perform in some way. It's time for my trick.

When the next person gets close to the box I toss a pad and pencil over the wall. I tell him to draw a letter of the alphabet without letting me see. Then I stare into his eyes, stroke my magical goatee and write on my own pad. He shows me his. It says "A". I show him mine, it says "A". It works! I do it over and over for people. Some are amazed, some merely amused, but none can doubt my Blaine-like powers.

I don't actually know how Blaine does this trick. Perhaps he really does read minds, or maybe he hypnotises people into writing whatever he wants. I don't do it that way. I just wait until they show me the pad, and then I write my answer using a tiny stub of pencil lead glued to my left thumb. It took a while to get it to stick, but it's not as if I had anything better to do.

3.10pm I ring the features department and attempt to negotiate an early release. There is a long pause at the other end. "We want to take more pictures of you first. It would be nice to get some more pictures, don't you think?" I don't hear any more from them. I've lost control of the situation.

4.38pm I'm beginning to hear this weird sound, as if the Perspex is itself resonating with ghostly music. I start to take things out of my rucksack one by one and listen to them, until I realise how that would look to anyone staring out of their office window.

5.45pm After several more calls someone finally agrees to come down to open the box. I am free. The experiment was a failure in one sense, in that I gave up two hours and 15 minutes shy of the 24-hour mark, but that's still a personal best, and I think I got a taste of what Blaine will experience in his first day suspended over the Thames: the discomfort, the boredom and the feeling of being a wholly unedifying public spectacle.

There are a few theories about how I coped with my bodily functions in the box. Some say I used the water bottle I'd brought in with me. Others say I peed through a tiny hole in the box itself. Still others say I loosened one wall using a concealed screwdriver and snuck into the loos nearest the delivery entrance. The latter theory remains the most popular, especially among those sceptics who, shortly after I began my ordeal, claim to have spotted me in a nearby pub. Believe, or don't believe. I've given away enough secrets for one day.

You Are the Story ...

To: reporter@NOTW.co.uk
Fr: mark@flipsidesolutions.com
Thanks for getting back to me. As per our telephone conversation, I am happy for you to run the orgy pix so long as you don't print anything about drugs. My client will be happy to pose for any orgy pix you might need, and the prostitutes will all be available for interviews at your convenience. I'm thrilled we were able to work this out – you're getting a great story, but it's paramount that I can trust you on this. Remember: no cocaine. What was your name again?

To: mark@flipsidesolutions.com
Fr: reporter@NOTW.co.uk
Hi mark. Thanks for the email. I'm sorry to tell you that I taped our last telephone conversation, and after careful consideration we have decided to run it as a page one splash in the NOTW this Sunday. As of now, you are the story. I hope this isn't too inconvenient.

To: reporter@NOTW.co.uk
Fr: mark@flipsidesolutions.co.uk

Just got your email. I was more or less expecting this, which is why I am happy to report that the drugs thing was a hoax. We staged it with a lookalike and some talcum powder for a new BBC series on the sleazy way in which tabloids engineer stories, which my client is presenting. Our phone calls and this correspondence will form the centrepiece of programme 1. So actually, you are the story. Do let me know if you need anything else.

To: mark@flipsidesolutions.com
Fr: reporter@NOTW.co.uk

We've known about your programme for months. Eva, who is pretending to be your assistant producer, is actually our work-experience girl. She replaced the talc with real cocaine halfway through filming, which is why it took your client 36 takes to do his piece to camera after he left, and why he's back in rehab now. Who is the story? YOU are the story.

To: reporter@NOTW.co.uk
Fr: mark@flipsidesolutions.com

Hi. Sorry not get back to you straight away. I just showed your last email to the police and they are coming to your office to arrest you for supplying a controlled substance. I've also spoken

to a rival newspaper, which is going to run the whole story
(which you are, btw) tomorrow.

To: mark@flipsidesolutions.com
Fr: reporter@NOTW.co.uk
Guess what! I'm not even a reporter, I'm just a 14-year-old kid
who hacked into the newspaper's email system!!! So maybe
YOU ARE THE STORY NOW DUMBASS

To: reporter@NOTW.co.uk
Fr: mark@flipsidesolutions.com
Darren, that u?

To: mark@flipsidesolutions.com
Fr: reporter@NOTW.co.uk
Kevin?

Welcome to the NewsRoom at permachat.co.uk, the UK's premier online
current affairs forum!

>connecting to server...
Current Host: Zoran1
Current Topic: New-style smart chip credit cards have reduced
    card fraud for the first time in nine years, leading to warn-
    ings that "identity theft", already rising, will become more

attractive to fraudsters. Are our identities safe anymore? What do you think?

capitalistpiglet: it's getting easier to lose your identity these days

Pashmina: not if u beleive in urself

capitalistpiglet: our credit cards are more sophisticated, but the documentation on which our identities are based remains vulnerable

Pashmina: just keep saying i am me

nameless: A NATIONAL ID CARD WOULD SOLVE THE PROBLEM

LadeezMan has entered the NewsRoom

LadeezMan: morning

Pashmina: hi ladeezman u still at the airport

capitalistpiglet: I'm not sure it would

LadeezMan: yes

Host_Zoran1: sticking to topic pliz

LadeezMan: whos zoran1

Pashmina: hes from slovankia

Host_Zoran1: helo. topic is identity thef

nameless: OF COURSE IT WOULD

LadeezMan: weres Chris2

Pashmina: on holiday. is yr flite goin soon

LadeezMan: dont know dont care

Host_Zoran1: sticking to topic pliz

Pashmina: ?????

LadeezMan: I like it here. The bars open v early

capitalistpiglet: even if ID cards did work, would it be worth the loss of freedom?

Pashmina: u r instatutionalised!!!

nameless: FREEDOM IS JUST ANOTHER WORD FOR BEING A SOFT TOUCH

capitlistpiglet: did you make that up?

Pashmina: no its a word!

Host_Zoran1: not sticking topic is geting kick out

capitalistpiglet: not you pash

Pashmina: maybe I didnt spell it right

LadeezMan: sometimes u wanna go were eveybody knows yr name

Pashmina: me spellins terrible

nameless: A SOFT TOUCH FOR FREELOADING IMMI-GRANTS

nameless has been kicked out of the NewsRoom

Host_Zoran1: he was not saying topic so he ban

Pashmina: Zoran1 u r soooo funny!!!!

Bronco has entered the NewsRoom

Host_Zoran1: I thank

Bronco: yo

Pashmina: hi bronc how was yr month on corfu

Host_Zoran1: all saying topic now pliz

Bronco: not corfu. curfew

Pashmina: I ALREADY SAID I CANT SPELL

>connection to server has been terminated...

This Week's Headlines

- **Unspecified Act Alleged** Two unnamed persons have allegedly done something. We cannot tell you who they are, but their pictures have been used to illustrate an unrelated article somewhere on this page. Can you find them?

- **Websites Named** Today we print the internet addresses of some very interesting websites where people speak freely on a number of issues. Have a look, then come back and reread the story on the previous page. It will suddenly make a lot more sense.

- **Unspecified Act Denied** A person who cannot be named for legal reasons has secretly denied participating in an alleged act that cannot be described for legal reasons. But you know who we mean.

- **Prince Charles Wears Sunglasses, Walks About, Chats To Strangers** If you don't know why this is interesting, then you need to go back to that website again. See?

- **Unnamed Denier Accidentally Names Self In Breach Of Injunction** For a minute there we thought we were on to something, but then the lawyers looked into it and decided it was better to be safe than sorry.

- **Footballers Again!** For now we'll just called them footballers A, B, C, D and E, and Damaging Allegations 1, 2 and 3. A is implicated in both 2 and 3 but not 1; C, D and E have played for England; B plays for a Premiership team that boasts four players allegedly interviewed by police over Allegation 1, although he himself is only in the frame for 3. Ask around the office. Someone will know.

- **John Leslie** We can name him all we like now, so long as we mention that he was cleared.
- **Unnamed Witness To Unspecified Act Alleged To Be Unnamed Person** Be careful – this is a different unspecified act, but some of the alleged participants are the same. Actually this is a really good story, but until the judge turns his mobile back on we can't even tell you how many people are involved: it could be TWO, or less than TWO or even more than TWO. See the picture of those TWO men on the next page? That's interesting, don't you think?
- **Fresh Allegations Fail To Surface** It's really ironic when you think about it. We know who we're talking about, and you know who we're talking about, and yet we still can't print anything. No, we've said too much already. You'll just have to wait for tomorrow's ruling. In the meantime, here's a picture of Paul Burrell looking shifty, and some space to jot down any spurious internet allegations you come across. Web addresses follow.

Tasers on Stun, Everybody

As a consequence of being burgled last week, the MP David Davies (not the shadow home secretary; that's Davis) wants all homeowners to be issued with Tasers. This may sound like an understandable overreaction on the part of someone who has been the victim of a crime, but Davies is prone to take things a bit too far. His response to the current sentencing crisis is a campaign called Stop All Forms of Early Release (Safer). Perhaps he couldn't afford to be more measured for fear of spoiling his acronym. I can sympathise with that. He's trying to make a name for himself. With someone else's name.

I was also burgled last week, in remarkably similar circumstances: front window forced open, mobiles and credit cards snatched, crime not discovered until morning. The Davies family lost their passports and the thieves stole their car and torched it – while the Dowlings argued about who left the window wide open all night before an alternative scenario presented itself. In fact, my kids are still blissfully unaware of the crime. (Don't worry, they'll never look here.)

The Taser idea is, to be fair, not as bad as my initial plan, which was to abandon domestic use of the ground floor and fill it knee-deep with poisonous snakes. Comments on the Daily Mail website are running almost 100 per cent in favour of Davies' proposal; unfortunately most respondents are labouring under the misapprehension that the other David Davis is its author. How galling.

I'm not in favour of handing out Tasers, although if everybody's getting one then I certainly want mine. The drawbacks are obvious. The non-lethal nature of the Taser – it causes nothing more than extreme pain, uncontrollable muscle contractions, collapse and temporary paralysis – comes with a corresponding moral equivalency. I don't want to kill anybody, but I can think of a few people I'd like to Taserise.

The Taser itself looks remarkably like a toy, and I'm sure ours would accidentally end up in the box where we keep all our space weaponry. Before you know it an ordinary pre-bedtime light sabre duel ends with Dad flopping around on the floor like a salmon. There's no established etiquette for mishaps. If I accidentally shoot 50,000 volts through a neighbour, is an apology enough, or do I have to go round with a bottle of wine? If he then shoots me, are we quits, or should I escalate?

Anyway, a Taser wouldn't have helped me or Davies because neither of us woke up. In hindsight I think we both did the right thing. It saves one having to make the terrible ethical choice between cowering in fear or getting beat up. This sort of burglar wants you to be home because he's after precisely those items – phone, wallet, iPod – you take with you when you go out. He doesn't wish to wake you, but he may well be prepared for that eventuality. Before we arm homeowners, let's remember that burglary is down by more than 30 per cent since 1997, while violent crime is rising nicely already. There has to be a better way. What's the biggest sheet of flypaper you can buy?

War & Peace

Welcome to the NewsRoom at permachat.co.uk, the UK's premiere online current affairs forum!

>connecting to server...

Current Host: Chris2

Current Topic: According to George Bush, US intelligence has found links between the Iraqi regime and al-Qaida. Does Saddam Hussein pose a terrorist threat, or is this "evidence" just another attempt to justify war? What do you think?

jenni@boughtledger: war is stupid

Host_Chris2: I think you've said it enough times now, jenni@

LadeezMan: 146

Bronco: saying war is stupid is stupid

jenni@boughtledger: war is stupid

LadeezMan: 147

Bronco: becos war is cool

capitalistpiglet: I know you all think you know what I'm going to say next...

Bronco: wait

Host_Chris2: at least we're sticking to the topic

Bronco: is it about muffins

capitalistpiglet: ...that this war is all about oil & Bush settling old scores

jenni@boughtledger: war is stupid

LadeezMan: 148

Bronco: muffins just popped into me head then. Like esp
Host_Chris2: I'm not sure the counting adds much, LadeezMan
LadeezMan: but he wasn't going to say muffins
capitalistpiglet: actually I do believe that military action could be justified on humanitarian grounds
jenni@boughtledger: war is stupid
Bronco: the feeling was so strong – MUFFINS
LadeezMan: its not ESP if he doesn't say muffins! 149
capitalistpiglet: but the US agenda is about securing oil fields not protecting the Iraqi people
Host_Chris2: anyone have a comment about piglet's comment?
jenni@boughtledger: war is stupid
Host_Chris2: you've made your point, jenni@. Anyone else?
LadeezMan: 150. Go girl
capitalistpiglet: this war will be fought for the wrong reasons
Bronco: it was like a deja vue
LadeezMan: except he still aint said muffins
jenni@boughtledger: war is stupid
LadeezMan: 151
Host_Chris2: ENOUGH. I do not want anyone else saying "war is stupid" OR counting, even in protest. ANYONE who does will be BANNED.
Pashmina has entered the NewsRoom
Pashmina: hi room
LadeezMan: hi
Pashmina: hi LadeezMan wots new

jenni@boughtledger has left the NewsRoom
LadeezMan: nothin
Pashmina: bit quiet in ere innit
Host_Chris2: Pashmina, are you worried about the threat of war?
Pashmina: war is stupid
LadeezMan: 152
Bronco: that is so wierd
Pashmina: hang on I dropped me muffin

>connection to server has been terminated...

The Trench

Settling down on my stool a few hours after sunset, I shone my candle on the floor of the dark, trickling trench, where I found the pencil stub I'd dropped earlier. Pulling a scrap of paper from my coat, I started to write a letter to my wife, which I dated March 1917. "Dearest Sophie," it began, "if only you could turn the kitchen television so it faces the window more, I too might be able to get a glimpse of EastEnders." I never finished that letter. Instead I slumped back against the mud wall, gazed up at the strip of threatening sky overhead and thought of home, which now seemed a world away, but was in fact 11 steps north.

The Trench, the BBC series in which 24 volunteers from Hull spend a fortnight reliving the horror of the first world war, has already garnered a lot of criticism. More than one commentator has opined that an Auschwitz re-enactment will be next, but I imagine the Japanese PoW camp will come first, followed by a series in which volunteers spend a few weeks in a dented plane in the Andes pretending to eat each other.

Of course the BBC is only trying to make history come alive, to lend the past the sensory element it has always lacked. Sadly they could not give their Hull volunteers a full and authentic experience of life in a frontline trench. They couldn't shoot them, for a start, or even wound them very much. They weren't allowed to give them dysentery. All in all, living in the trench was probably safer than staying behind in Hull. The BBC could only provide the volunteers with two weeks of painfully accurate privation, down a period hole. Viewers, of course, won't even get this much; we'll only be able to watch other people going through it. Even at its best, reality TV is still just TV. This is why I decided to spend some time in my own first-world-war trench. Of course I could never really experience anything like what veterans of the trenches went through, which is good, because I wouldn't want to. But I thought I might be able to get just an inkling of what it might be like to participate in a BBC re-enactment.

The BBC's trench was 60 yards long and dug into a field near Cambrai in France. For technical reasons to do with the dimensions of my back garden, my trench was slightly less than full scale: just nine feet long, a mere cross section. James, the man who dug it for me, did a beautiful job: nice straight sides sliced into the wet London clay, with a little set of steps at one end. By piling the extracted clay up on either side of the trench he was able to achieve an impressive depth, but he warned me not stay in it for too long if it rained. The walls, he said, would slide in on me.

The next morning I prepared my trench for habitation. About three inches of water had collected in it overnight, leaking in from the oozing clay walls. The bottom step was already subsiding into the mire. Trenches, it seems, are far from ideal under any circumstances. Whose idea were they? I bailed it out as best I could, dug a little drainage channel for the water, and put some old boards over the top of it. This gave me a dry floor, but the trench was still dank, smelly and suffused with an unholy chill. So far, so realistic. I went to get dressed.

Having been hastily collected over the course of the previous day, my kit was not strictly historically accurate: my coat was Russian, my gas mask Belgian and my helmet from the wrong war. "What's it for? A fancy-dress party?" asked the man at the army surplus shop. How to explain? "Yes," I said.

Once on, however, the costume was heavy, authentically itchy and rather too much for early March. Into the trench I put a little child's folding chair for a camp stool and an old crate for a table. I began the day by "standing to": looking out for enemy movement in the direction of no man's land, just past the shed, and then sat down to enjoy a carefully measured morning rum ration (two tablespoons exactly). After that I flipped through my rather thin collection of first world war literature – a small book of poetry, Sebastian Faulks's Birdsong, Ben MacIntyre's A Foreign Field, Pat Barker's The Ghost Road – trying to summon up fear, depression and shellshock.

Time in the trench passed very slowly. I had neglected to bring a watch down with me, but I could see the kitchen clock easily enough if I stood up. Unfortunately, standing up also gave the neighbours a good view of me peeking out of a trench in the middle of my back garden wearing a helmet and a gas mask. This was incentive enough for me to keep my head down for most of the day. I ate some rough French bread and ladled out some drinking water from my meagre supply. Worms crawled out of the walls, looked at me, and crawled back in.

At about four my sons arrived home from school. They raided my trench and stole my bread, before taking up their positions. I had already instructed them to chuck handfuls of sand on me (from a pail I'd filled earlier) at random intervals in order to simulate nearby explosions. They performed this duty with rather too much relish, and I was forced to make a rule about how far away they had to stand. The overall effect was, if not exactly terrifying, fairly bad for morale. When the sand ran out, large clods of earth started raining down on my head. Then came a barrage of gravel and plastic toys. A watering can made a direct hit, knocking everything off my makeshift table. One of my precious rum miniatures disappeared into the mud. I shouted at them to stop, but they just laughed.

Then my wife's head appeared. "Can you just tell me what your plans are?" she asked testily. "I mean, are you sleeping in there tonight?" I told her I didn't know yet. This sent her into a fury. She had not been at all supportive about the trench. She didn't care if history came alive for me. As far as she was concerned I was just pissing about in a big hole in the lawn when I was supposed to be taking Barnaby to his swimming lesson. To spare further argument, I volunteered for the mission. Secretly, I was glad to go.

Back in the real world, the stupidity of my experiment was thrown into sharp relief. What insight could I hope to gain from spending a day doing something mildly unpleasant? I'm not even being filmed while I'm doing it. And what's so great about the tragic past anyway? How about the tragic present? After all, there are plenty of places one can go today to experience wholly authentic fear, disease and death. It's not as if we've got rid of war.

After the swimming lesson I returned dutifully to my trench. It was dark by now, with oily water lapping around the floorboards. I lit a candle stub, which flickered in the damp breeze. After their baths the children came down into the trench in their pyjamas, bringing piles of newspaper to sit on. It was the perfect opportunity to indulge in a little trench camaraderie. With any luck, they might even give me lice. While they stared into the guttering flame I told them stories of men standing waist-high in freezing water for weeks at a time, of rats as big as cats, of a war that was meant to end all war.

"I'm getting more biscuits," said one.

"Don't get Dad any. He's not allowed," said another.

"I like fire," said the third.

After they went to bed, I tried to read more war poetry, but I was too distracted by the trickling of the walls. Instead I slipped into a miserable sulk while flagrantly exceeding my rum ration. There was so much that I had failed to achieve in my short time below ground. At some point, for example, I had intended to shave with a genuine first world war-era Gillette safety razor, using cold water, before a mud-splattered shard of mirror, but I'd forgotten and now it was too dark. Luckily there weren't any BBC people around to issue period punishments for such disciplinary infractions. With no one to police me, I'd allowed lots of little inaccuracies and anachronisms to creep into my day, some historically justifiable, some less so. When I left the trench to go inside and heat up some soup in the middle of the afternoon, I justified it by pretending that I was on routine patrol, raiding a small, abandoned farmhouse behind the lines. I probably shouldn't have stayed to watch 15 to 1, but on reflection I don't think it detracted from the experience too much.

When the rum ran out at about 10.30pm, I had to make a decision about whether I was going to sleep in the trench. My first world war camp bed was still in the kitchen. It wouldn't fit in the trench unless I took out the table and the chair first, so there would have to be a historical time-out while I reconfigured things. But it was cold and I was covered in mud. My ears were full of dirt. The puddle at the bottom of the trench had risen up over the boards and flooded my boots. The tails of my coat had been underwater for some time. The neighbour's cat was staring at me from the top of the garden wall. While I dithered, a light rain began to fall. I remembered what James had said about rain, about the trench sliding in on me while I slept, and I prayed for it to rain a little harder so I could abandon the experiment in good conscience. The rain stopped. I stood up and looked at the kitchen clock: 11.30pm. I thought I had better stick it out for at least a few more hours, so as not to cheat myself of the suffering endured by those brave BBC volunteers. Then I thought: "Sod this for a game of soldiers – I'm deserting."

Welcome to the NewsRoom at permachat.co.uk, the UK's premiere online current affairs forum!

>connecting to server...

Current Host: Chris5

Current Topic: Tony Blair has promised to publish a dossier of evidence against Saddam Hussein in the coming weeks, to make the case for attacking Iraq. Meanwhile, American tanks are already being moved to the Iraqi border in Kuwait. Is war with Iraq now a foregone conclusion? What do you think?

jenni@boughtledger: WAR

Bronco: war!

jenni@boughtledger: good god, y'all!

Bronco: wot is it good for!

nameless: it's good for the economy

Bronco: is it

nameless: it drives oil prices up in the short tErm, while protecting the free flow of crude oil in the long term

jenni@boughtledger: say it again!

nameless: it also provides an important proving ground for new military technology

Bronco: 2 much info now

Pashmina has entered the NewsRoom

Bronco: wb pash

Pashmina: room

jenni@boughtledger: WAR

Pashmina: you 2 still singin I see

Bronco: yes. WAR

nameless: is the only way to prevent Saddam from developing nuclear weapons

LADEEZMAN has entered the NewsRoom

LADEEZMAN: how do I look

Bronco: wikked! u capped up yr username!!

Pashmina: it siuts you

jenni@boughtledger: WAR

nameless: is simply diplomacy by other means

Bronco: who IS this guy

nameless: I am nameless

Pashmina: thats not alowwed. you must have a name

nameless: my name is nameless

Pashmina: throw him out Chris2

Bronco: where is Chris2?

Pashmina: Chris2, WERE ARE YOU

Host_Chris5: hes not here

Pashmina: WERE IS HE THEN

Host_Chris5: hes away

Pashmina: well pls throw out nameless for having no name NOW

Host_Chris5: his name is nameless

LADEEZMAN: well tell him to stick to the topic

Host_Chris5: he is

Pashmina: Chris5 u need 2 be a little more pro activ I think

Host_Chris5: whatever

Bronco: how come they skipped Chris3 and Chris4

LADEEZMAN: its annarchy in ere

jenni@boughtledger: i'm a celebrity get me out here!

jenni@boughtledger has left the NewsRoom

Pashmina: she must think shes lara tomkins-palmerson or summat

Host_Chris5: the next person who bothers me is banned

>connection to server has been terminated...

So Where Were You?

In the wake of the anniversary of the attack on the World Trade Centre, many journalists have written about where they were when the Towers were hit, and how it affected them. Space prevented us printing every single searing account last week, but here we present the final six.

- **The tabloid reporter** It was a typical day on the news desk. I was changing into my Harry Potter costume when the news came in. After the initial shock, I started to change back into my own clothes, but then someone said I should keep the costume on until the editor had had a chance to laugh at me. It was a terrible, terrible day. I was so stressed out.

- **The freelance journalist** I was at home working on an article about towels. I turned on the television for my afternoon fix of Watercolour Challenge, and when I saw what was happening, I realised right there and then that nobody was going to care about towels for a while. The editor made me finish it anyway (of course!), but they never ran it. They paid me half my fee, which, under the circumstances, was absolutely disgusting.

- **The photographer** A bunch of us were staked out at Liam Gallagher's house – it was recycling day, and he's usually fairly conscientious about that sort of thing. It's a side of him a lot of people don't see. But he never came out. We knew something was wrong.

- **The intern** Tony Blair was going to speak at the TUC conference. The year before, he got these big sweat stains, so we were all on full Underarm Alert to see if he would repeat the performance. For obvious reasons, we never found out. I had £50 on it as well.
- **The deputy showbiz correspondent** I remember it like it was yesterday. I left the pub at about 2pm, and it was only when I got back to the office that I realised I'd left my tape recorder behind, with the tape of the interview I'd just done with Ant and Dec still in it! Initially when it happened, I wanted to go straight back to the pub and get it, but it seemed sort of inappropriate at that stage. So I sat down and wrote up the interview from memory, which wasn't easy. I went back to the pub a few days later, but by then the tape recorder was gone.
- **The short contract staffer** White chocolate was about to be the new black – of course nobody remembers that now – so we were doing a big spread called The White Stuff. I couldn't get anyone on the phone; it just seemed so odd that no one wanted to talk about white chocolate! When I realised what had happened, I thought, "I can't just give up on the chocolate piece. I mean, that's just what these terrorists want". It was very difficult to keep ringing people for recipes, but I instinctively knew it was the right thing to do.

Singalonga-Kim

North Korea's Communist party newspaper urged the country's people on Monday to redouble their courage and sing the song "Long Trip for Army-based Leadership" more loudly at a time of tension with the United States. *Reuters*

Top 10 Songs for the Duration of the Staunch Struggle

1 **Good Riddance to the Expelled Inspectors of the International Atomic Energy Commission** This should be sung sonorously in order to bolster spirits for the coming conflict. Be advised that verse four, which begins, "Nuclear reprocessing is our birthright", goes up a half-step. Do not forget this.

2 **Your Evil Food Aid Cannot Destroy Our Faith In Juche** To be sung twice through while abstaining from lunch. Our cherished philosophy of self-reliance must burn vigilantly in our hearts at this testing time. Second chorus is ladies only.

3 **Dear Leader, How Do You Stay So Slim?** This is a new one, so you will need to learn the words without delay. For maximum efficiency and the convenience of all citizens, it is sung to the tune of Let's Farm Well This Year As Asked By the Rural Theses.

4 **Pyongyang in Springtime Is So Impregnable** This was number one last spring, so there are no excuses for lack of

lyric-knowledge or inharmoniousness. It's going on heavy rotation from next week. Just start singing when you hear it on the loudspeakers.

5 Juche, Juche, Juche (Everybody Dance) From Tuesday this is number four on the official karaoke list, replacing Let's Enrich the Communist Economy First With Rice.

6 Bush the Evil Cretin The words are on the back of your ration book. The decadent capitalist drug dirge Puff the Magic Dragon will be temporarily unbanned so that all Koreans may become accustomed to the appropriate melody. Do not attempt to translate the words. Those citizens with harmony parts will be notified by telegram.

7 Please Me By Dying for the Motherland, Soldier-Husband Very appropriate for weddings. The CD is in Department Store Number One now.

8 Come on, Fill the Quota (for Annual Anti-Tank Missile Production) Words and music by the Dear Leader. A debut performance by the Sea of Blood Opera Company will be broadcast at the weekend – don't-miss television at its most punishable.

9 Give Me More of That Delicious, Nutritious Soup Made From Grass Careful, it's in swing time, so it needs to be sung with plenty of juche. There will be fines for all who do not successfully follow the appropriate rhythmic clapping procedure.

10 Me and Bobby McGee Still hanging in there.

Covering the War: Tips and Tricks

- **Sky News correspondent** "We were heading north on the road to Diwaniya when I was forced to take charge of the tank, because we were losing the light. In the end I said shell anything – anything! – and make it look like you mean it. Luckily, a little convoy of vehicles came into view just before the 3 o'clock bulletin. I wanted to do a second take, but war just isn't like that."

- **BBC News 24 cameraman** "Sometimes, especially first thing in the morning, a sandstorm just doesn't look like a sandstorm. On TV everything appears to be perfectly normal. You have this idiot banging on about zero visibility when the viewer can clearly see a burning skyline in the background. So what I do is, I point the camera at the ground and tell the reporter to lie on his back underneath it. You have to play with the depth of field a bit, but it works pretty well."

- **ITN correspondent** "You never know what's going to happen while you're reporting live while under fire, so you have to be prepared for every contingency. The first time you forget to put the nappy on, that's when something's going to go wrong."

- **Channel 5 presenter** "I sit on a plate of gravel. It helps me do the concerned face when I'm actually thinking about lunch."

- **Channel 4 reporter** "I have a special 'on air' gas mask, which comes from an Action Man Halloween costume. To be honest, no one can understand a word you're saying when you're wearing the real thing. And 'sand goggles' are actually just ski goggles. There are some very good end-of-season deals just now, so shop around."

- **BBC correspondent** "You have to keep your wits about you at all times. If you fall asleep for two seconds Rageh Omaar will tie your shoelaces together and then shout 'Gas Gas Gas!' in your ear. He's not the Mr Nice Guy you see on the screen."

- **Al-Jazeera reporter** "If you haven't got a huge budget, then forget about the big explosions; concentrate on the dead bodies. Nobody else is doing dead bodies right now, which is why we have the edge."

- **CNN producer** "If the war isn't going your way, don't hesitate to complain on air. They're never going to direct combat in a media-friendly fashion unless we make it clear that we're extremely disappointed by the lack of progress so far. Also, don't order the Kid Meal at the Kuwait City Burger King, unless you like baby goat."

Lend Us Your Minds

Today on Towards Freedom TV: Serving Free Iraq from aboard the "Commando Solo" C-130 Hercules transport plane

7am: Good Morning with Rashid and Uday A lively mix of prayers, chat and fashion, plus tips on boiling drinking water.

9am: A Message From President George W Bush Pre-recorded address to the Iraqi people, in English with Arabic subtitles. Sincere assurances of America's purest intentions.

9.15am: A Message From Tony Blair More friendly overtures.

9.30am: Don't Loot Hour-long public-service exhortation.

10.30am: The Fresh Prince of Nasiriya Sitcom about an exiled opposition leader who makes an emotional return to his homeland at the behest of the US State Department. Gentle, informative hilarity from the writers of Avoid Downed Power Lines.

11am: Checkpoint and Roadblock Etiquette Practical advice on how to avoid being shot.

12am: The Christianity Hour Inspirational faith-based programme in which ordinary Iraqis convert to Christianity, receiving in return the everlasting love of Jesus Christ, snacks and blankets.

12.30pm: Refuelling Break Transmission resumes at 1pm.

1pm: News Latest liberty update from Corporal Ron Jenks of the 173rd Airborne Brigade.

2pm: Humanitarian Aid Roadshow Today the roadshow team bring their water trucks to the outskirts of Basra.

3.30pm: Farewell Bad Dictator After years of censorship, Iraqis can at last phone in and say bad things about Saddam Hussein on live TV, subject to the telecommunications network being restored in your area.

4:30pm: Iraq's Funniest Home Videos More hilarious broken statues, torn posters and trashed palaces.

5pm: Messages From George Bush and Tony Blair For those whose electricity supplies may have been disrupted during the day, another opportunity to catch these messages of genuine affection and support.

5.30pm: Refuelling Break

6pm: News and weather From the Towards Freedom news team.

7.30pm: Public Service TV A short film, Watch Out for Loose or Falling Masonry, narrated by NBA legend Michael Jordan.

8pm: Will and Grace Sensitively dubbed American comedy series about a handsome young lawyer, his beautiful wife and the mentally retarded child-man they have adopted.

8:30pm: Ground Forces Baghdad Special A large area to the north-west of the city is completely relandscaped by a team from 3rd Infantry Division.

9pm: News Headlines followed by tonight's Curfew Film, Columbo: Blueprint for Murder (1972).

11pm: Messages from George Bush and Tony Blair A last chance to catch these heartfelt reassurances.

Welcome to the NewsRoom at permachat.co.uk, the UK's premiere online current affairs forum!

>connecting to server...

Current Host: Chris2

Current Topic: The deaths of Uday and Qusay Hussein have prompted celebrations across Iraq, but do they represent a turning point for the coalition's postwar efforts, or is the news just a well-timed bit of political propaganda? What do you think?

Pashmina: its sad innit

LadeezMan: no its happy

USABob: ITS GREAT NEWS

capitalistpiglet: Iraq needs stability, not shootouts in the street.

Bronco has entered the NewsRoom

Pashmina: you can't be happy when some1 gets killed even if there bad!!!!!

Bronco: who got killed

capitalistpiglet: Uday & Qusay

LadeezMan: they were evil!

Bronco: the cheeky girls are dead?

USABob: THEYRE SADDAM HUSSEINS SONS YOU PINHEAD

Host_Chris2: caps off please

capitalistpiglet: the question is, what do the coalition forces do now?

USABob: KILL SADDAM

Host_Chris2: caps off please

zam-zam has entered the NewsRoom

zam-zam: bonjour

Pashmina: wot

Host_Chris2: bonjour zam-zam. Aujourd'hui le sujet c'est le futur d'Iraq. Votre avis?

LadeezMan: Chris2 i didnt know you coud speak italian

Host_Chris2: c'est le francais, LadeezMan

zam-zam: ou est les <<big tits>>, svp

Pashmina: eveyone speak english please

Host_Chris2: pardon?

zam-zam: Pashmina avez-vous des <<big tits>>? J'ai une erection enormee.

Pashmina: wots he sayin to me!!!!

capitalistpiglet: you don't want to know

LadeezMan: I do

Host_Chris2: zam-zam, le langage injurieux est formellement interdit par la politique de cette chatroom.

USABob: I DONT LIKE THE SOUND OF IT ONE BIT

Host_Chris2: caps off please

zam-zam: c'est spermchat.co.uk, non?

USABob: IM SORRY THE BUTTON IS STUCK

Host_Chris2: non, c'est permachat.co.uk, une tribune pour discuter des evenements actuel.

zam-zam: je suis desolé

zam-zam has left the NewsRoom

Pashmina: asta la vista
Bronco: bloody asylum seekers

>*connection to server has been terminated...*

PermaBlog – Non-stop comment for a non-stop planet!

T. Dennis LaForche – Victory in Iraq: If We Believe We Can Win, We Already Have

Recently a former State Department official said that the war in Iraq was not winnable, "in any sense of the word 'winnable'", which shows how his vocabulary, like his attitude, has become limited by negative thinking. Everything is "winnable", in every sense of the word, as long as we take care to extract only what is positive from a given outcome. The situation in Baghdad, to the untrained eye ... *[read more]*

Posted by TDennisLaForche at 1202 today

T. Dennis LaForche is the author of Frag the Fear: Success Secrets of the Swift Boat Veterans

COMMENTS

I don't understand. Is this guy actually suggesting that we can achieve victory through neuro-linguistic programming?
SixKindsOfChris at 1232 today

hi chris. Your comments are always so clever!!
JaneT at 1304 today

I don't know I didn't read it. T. Dennis LaForche – What begins with T that's worse than Dennis?
ElSmell at 1315 today

---

if i am want to wear the veal it is my choose
SE14 at 1322 today

Hi Janet. Thanks.
SixKindsOfChris at 1329 today

You may think it's your choice, SE14, but the wearing of the veil is still a symbol of the oppression of women, IMHO.
liberati at 1336 today

The T stands for Theodore and what does the wearing of veils have to do with my thesis? You people aren't debating the right points!
TDennisLaForche at 1340 today

---

my name's not Janet, it's Jane T, 36, single, from suffolk. Chris: I really liked that thing you said on your website about the "bumbling aggression of US foreign policy" 3 years ago.
Janet at 1347 today

You had your blog Tdennis so piss off out of the comments section. This is OURS

ElSmell at 1355 today

I am a man so is ok

SE14 at 1402 today

Hang on, SE14 – so are you actually wearing veal?

liberati at 1404 today

AGREED THE EXIT STRATEGY ON IRAQ NEEDS RETHINKING BUT THIS IS NOT THE SAME AS LOSING NOR IS IT ANOTHER VIETNAM AND EVEN IF IT IS WE CAN WIN THIS ONE AS LONG AS WE COMMIT OURSELVES ONE HUNDRED PER CENT TO THE LONG STRUGGLE AHEAD. THIS IS NOT THE TIME TO BACK DOWN

SPECIALRELATIONSHIP at 1414 today

Erm, thanks jane. You seem to know a lot about me

SixKindsOfChris at 1417 today

Is "farm assured" so is ok

SE14 at 1421 today

Everything but your address. But I'm working on it! Just kidding
Janet at 1424 today

You must be registered to post a comment

The
End

Welcome to the NewsRoom at permachat.co.uk, the UK's premier online current affairs forum! Now with emoticons!

>*connecting to server...*

Current Host: Chris2

Current Topic: Disaster relief in New Orleans in the wake of hurricane Katrina has been derided as too little, too late, but who is to blame? What do you think? Add a dash of verve to your comments with our new emoticons!

capitalistpiglet: it's truly tragic

Bronco: ☺

Pashmina has entered the NewsRoom

Host_Chris2: do you mean the disaster itself or the mishandled relief operation?

Pashmina: hi room

capitalistpiglet: I mean these emoticons. Hi pash

Pashmina: wot is emoticons

Bronco: ☺

capitalistpiglet: that

Host_Chris2: I was against them, but they've now been rolled out across the site

Pashmina: how u do it

LadeezMan has entered the NewsRoom

Bronco: hi ladeezman hows u

LadeezMan: ☺

Bronco: 😁

capitalistpiglet: they impoverish debate

Pashmina: ☺

Bronco: ☺

Pashmina: LOL

Host_Chris2: I agree

Pashmina: sorry I mean 😁

LadeezMan: 😐

capitalistpiglet: this is completely moronic

LadeezMan: 😉

Bronco: 😁

Host_Chris2: let's try to address the topic. Pashmina, what do you think of the Katrina disaster?

Pashmina: 🙁

capitalistpiglet: that's it? 10,000 dead and your response is a sad face?

Pashmina: 🙁🙁🙁🙁

Bronco: 😁

Host_Chris2: aren't you angry about the way the relief operation was handled?

Pashmina: yes but there aint no face for that

capitalistpiglet: it's clear the federal govt ignored all warnings

Pashmina: oh hang on 😟

Bronco: 😁

capitalistpiglet: I'm going to stop coming here

Pashmina: ligthen up piglet its only a bit of fun ☺

capitalistpiglet: 😐

Pashmina: u do one Chris2. They're cute! ☺

Host_Chris2: I don't see one that expresses how I feel

Bronco: scroll down theres loads 😀

LadeezMan: 😎

Host_Chris2: how's this: 😕

Pashmina: 😀😀😀

>*connection to server has been terminated...*